KU-585-193

Musée de l'Orangerie

The Nymphéas
of Claude Monet

Michel Hoog

Musée de l'Orangerie
The Nymphéas
of Claude Monet

Réunion
des Musées
Nationaux

The French edition of this book was awarded the Prix Bernier of the Institut de France.
The text of this third edition is the same
as the second (1989), but the bibliography has been revised (2006).

The titles of the decorative panels in the Orangerie raise a special problem. The only document validated by Monet which enables them to be given specific names is the deed of donation dated 12 April 1922 (see p.125), in which the entire set is referred to as "The Nymphéas Series" and each composition is given an individual title and a location marked on the Lefèvre plan of 20 January (see p.46). However, on the one hand, the indications in the deed partially contradict those marked on the plan, and, on the other hand, the final arrangement differed somewhat from that provided by the deed. Only the four compositions in the first room and, to a lesser extent, one of the four in the second (*Tree Reflections*) seem to correspond to the initial titles. Faced with these uncertainties, some writers have decided not to use any particular title. Daniel Wildenstein preferred to keep the titles in the deed of donation for the five compositions which can be clearly identified and to give new titles to the three compositions in the second room which obviously differ from those noted in the deed of donation. We have followed this policy for the captions to the illustrations in this edition, while distinguishing the five original titles with inverted commas.

P.G. 2006

Translated by Jean-Marie Clarke

Cover: "Morning", detail, p. 27-30
Paris, Musée de l'Orangerie

Frontispiece:
Claude Monet in his garden at Giverny,
Photograph by Sacha Guitry, 1918
Document Musée d'Orsay

ISBN 2-7118-5069-2
© Editions de la Réunion des musées nationaux, Paris 2006
© Adagp, Paris 2006

1989 edition with a revised bibliography (2006)
49, rue Etienne-Marcel, 75001 Paris

"The Nymphéas Series"
The entire set in the Orangerie (circa 1914-1926)

First room:
Four compositions in 10 panels, H. 200

"The Clouds"
Three adjoining panels, W. 425 each; i.e. total W. 1275.
Inv. 20100
"Morning"
Four adjoining panels, respectively W. 212.5; W. 425; W. 425; W. 212.5, i.e. total W. 1275
Inv. 20101
"Green Reflections"
Two adjoining panels, W. 425 each; i.e. total W. 1275
Inv. 20102
"Setting Sun"
One panel L. 600
Inv. 20103

Second room:
Four compositions in 12 panels of H. 200

"Tree Reflections"
Two adjoining panels W. 425; i.e. total W. 850
Inv. 20107
Morning with Willows
Three adjoining panels of W. 425 each, i.e. total W. 1,275
Inv. 20105
Clear Morning with Willows
Three adjoining panels of W. 425 each, i.e. total W. 1,275
Inv. 20106
The Two Willows
Four adjoining panels of W. 425 each, i.e. total W. 1,700
Inv. 20104

Table of contents

Introduction   6

The Garden   11

The Series of Water-Lilies   19

The Panels of the Orangerie   55

The Path to Abstraction   75

The Poetics of the Nymphéas   99

Appendix: documents   119
Micrographic analysis of the pigments and support   127
Identification of the principal pigments   127
Bibliography   128
Exhibitions   131
Index of names   132

Monet is the Michelangelo of our time.

MARC CHAGALL
(quoted by P. Schneider in *Les Dialogues du Louvre*,
Paris, 1967, p. 42)

Introduction

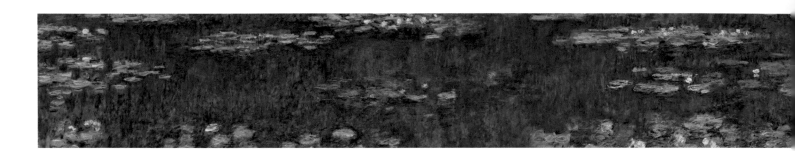

The word testament has so often been used to designate the last important works of artists and writers, that it is not without some hesitation that we use it here in speaking of the *Nymphéas* of Claude Monet. Yet this term has rarely been so appropriate. The eight panels of the *Nymphéas* are a monument to a long meditation and a long labor, and their specially designed installation in the Orangerie of the Tuileries, in the heart of Paris, was opened to the public only after the artist's death. Greeted with strong reactions from the outset, they became a constant source of inspiration for the generations to come.

The eight compositions of the Orangerie, mounted on the rounded walls of two oval rooms, all have the same height (2.97 m), but are of unequal length. The entire set, one of the most monumental realizations in painting of the first half of the 20th century, presents a total area of about 200 m².

The size of these painted surfaces and their disposition in an all-round presentation—enveloping the enthralled spectator in a sort of colored haze—have less impact in an age which has seen "*environments*" become a standard means of expression for artists. This, however, was not the case when they were first unveiled.

The abundance of the literature around the *Nymphéas* is somewhat deceptive, for as soon as Monet had shown the first panels to visitors, and even as soon as the exhibition of a first series in 1909 at Durand-Ruel's gallery had come to the attention of the more knowledgeable observers, the *Nymphéas* inspired commentaries which extended beyond the closed confines of art criticism. Those privileged enough to be invited to Giverny often wrote and published their impressions. And if certain remarks attributed to Monet may be found in more than one account, their tone and wording vary considerably; unfortunately, they probably inform us more about the personality of those who set them down than about the artist's actual words. In fact, Monet disliked expressing himself in writing; some of his later letters to Clemenceau, for example, deal more with his moods than with developing any thoughts. One of the rare texts signed by Monet and published during his lifetime (on Rodin at the Exposition of 1900) is nothing but an ironic pirouette.

The number of artists, writers, critics, and poets (Proust, Péguy, Bachelard, André Masson, Claudel, Ozenfant, to mention only a few) who set down their impressions of this unprecedented work is legion. Art historians—Anglo-Saxon for the most part—have tried to analyze its genesis, without always succeeding in elucidating the course of Monet's efforts.

We have also tried to relate in detail the history of the *Nymphéas*, starting with the recently reconstituted garden at Giverny (thanks to Mr. and Mrs. G. Van der Kemp), in which, as one early critic put it, "the artist himself created the subject of his inspiration" (Thiébault-Sisson, *Le Temps*, April 6, 1920). From the day of the Armistice in 1918, when Monet notified his friend Clemenceau[1] of his intention to donate "two panels" to the State, to the installation in 1927 of *eight* large compositions in the Orangerie, it is not always easy to follow the progress of the painter, who was discouraged by a cataract condition. The elaboration of the Orangerie panels themselves and Monet's often difficult relations with the Administration have given rise to contradictory accounts, sometimes misrepresenting the role of the public powers. Unfortunately, the archives are incomplete; but thanks to newly-discovered documents and a close study of existing material, we are able to present some new information. Certain parts of the story, however, have yet to be elucidated.

I would like to express my sincerest gratitude to Mssrs. and Mrs. Arizzoli-Clémentel, G. Barrelet-Clémentel, Y. Cantarel-Besson, Général de Cossé-Brissac, C. Durand-Ruel Besson, M. Fargeas, M. Garetta, N. Isaacson, J. de Ladoucette, M. Laurent, M. Linsay, F. Nourissier, C. Robert, M. Tendron, Me. Texier, G. Van der Kemp, N. Villa, R. Walter, D. Wildenstein, A. and M. Wormser, who facilitated my research, gave me access to information and previously unpublished documents, and authorized their publication.

B. David-Weill, P. Gillet, and S. Maignan lent me their precious assistance in putting this work into final form.

I would also like to thank D. Arnaudet and M. Bellot of the Service Photographique de la Réunion des musées nationaux for solving the difficult photographic problems posed by the *Nymphéas* because of their format and curvature.

The delicate task of restoration was carried out by F. Hourrière, assisted by C. Willoughby and T. Prunet, under the direction of S. Bergeon, Conservator, Head of the Service de la Restauration des Peintures des Musées Nationaux.

M.H.

1. Georges Clemenceau (1841-1929), a famous French statesman, was one of Monet's closest friends.

Étienne Clémentel
The water lilies at Giverny,
circa 1920
Paris, Musée d'Orsay

Étienne Clémentel
Monet standing by the water lilies at Giverny,
circa 1920
Paris, Musée d'Orsay

Étienne Clémentel
Path at Giverny,
circa 1920
Paris, Musée d'Orsay

*In this strange, dense garden, in this little paradise, famous, exotic and secret,
the fancy of a gardener and of a lover of water, in this little abnormal
world—greenhouse, forest, and aquarium—spanned by a Japanese-style footbridge
painted in bright green lacquer, the artist was to find the source of his most
incomparable inspirations. (…)*

*Will this work, one of the most daring ever attempted in painting,
be understood?*

LOUIS GILLET

The Garden

During his life, Monet never lived far from the Seine. After having spent his childhood at Le Havre, his youth in Paris, worked at Bougival, Argenteuil, lived in Vétheuil and Poissy, Monet himself admitted that he felt good only near the Seine. He often travelled to distant places, but never for long. In 1883, he rented a house at Giverny, between La Roche-Guyon and Vernon, in the department of the Eure, just at the edge of the former department of Seine-et-Oise. Nearby flowed a small arm of the Epte, the river traditionally considered as the border between the Normandy and the Ile-de-France regions. That he was enchanted by the countryside is beyond doubt—he said as much himself any number of times—but it should be noted that this move took him rather far from Paris, and also that it coincided with the dispersion of the Impressionist group. Renoir had recently settled in the Midi, and Sisley at Moret. Cézanne was spending more and more time at Aix-en-Provence. Monet's move corresponded to a similar tendency among his friends at that time;

and although they stayed in touch, the ties between them loosened somewhat. Without trying to make Monet a slave of geographic determinism, it could be said that there was nothing random about his decision, which soon proved to be definitive, to settle—at that particular point in his career, when he was at the peak of his powers, when his family situation was stabilizing, and his financial situation improving—precisely where his native Normandy began and not in Ile-de-France.

His stay at Poissy had left him dissatisfied; he did not like the environs and he had had problems with his landlord. A flood had disrupted his home life, and he wanted to find a "fixed place to settle down" (letter to Durand-Ruel of April 5, 1883). That same month he discovered Giverny, a village of 300 inhabitants, rented a house, and returned to Paris to attend Manet's funeral (he was one of the pallbearers, along with Antonin Proust, Zola, Duret, Fantin-Latour, A. Stevens, and P. Burty). On his return to Giverny, he set up his floating studios, but painted little; he wrote to Durand-Ruel that he first had to accustom himself to his new environment (letter of July 3, 1883), proof of his need first to absorb and assimilate the visual spectacle that surrounded him. In December, he travelled in the Midi with Renoir, visited Cézanne, and pushed as far as Bordighera and Menton. But this is not the time to follow Monet in all of his expeditions. It should only be noted that his settling down in Giverny was not immediate but progressive; until 1889, he was frequently absent from Giverny, and, later, his love for his garden and his house never prevented him from travelling around.

In 1889-1890, his material and psychological circumstances also changed. His joint exhibition with Rodin at the gallery of Georges Petit was a success, and his major role in the subscription campaign for the purchase of Manet's *Olympia* put him in the limelight. In November 1890, "certain of never finding a better installation or a more beautiful countryside" (letter of October 27, 1890 to Durand-Ruel, DW. no. 1078), he bought the property at Giverny that he had been renting for seven years, for 22,000 francs defrayable in four annual payments (by way of comparison, a legislator in Parliament at the time received an indemnity of 12,000 francs a year). After years of want and misery, Monet was finally well-off enough to live at his ease.

The deed of sale, dated November 19, is a precious document, for it gives us a detailed description of the house before Monet's modifications. The main house consisted of four rooms on the ground floor, as many on the first floor, a cellar, and an attic. Adjacent, to the west, was a sort of barn which Monet used as a studio. In front of the house ran the village street, and in the back, on a gentle slope, was a small garden (the whole formed an oblong with an area of roughly 2$^{1}/_{2}$ acres, see plan), bordered by a little-travelled road and railroad tracks. Monet worked in this flower-filled garden, whose first aspect we know from an article by Octave Mirbeau. He also painted in the environs as often as in his garden; this was the period of the series, first the *Poplars*, then the *Haystacks*, models for which were plentiful around the village. In 1892, he began the major series of the *Rouen Cathedral*, and married his companion, Alice Hoschédé (the wedding was held at Giverny). The year 1893 was a decisive one. He bought the plot of land lying between the railroad tracks and the Ru River, in the prolongation of his property (see plan p. 13). He also rented a third plot beyond the river, on the other side of the road and the railway. He immediately made plans to dig a pond for aquatic plants, to be fed by water drawn from the Epte at one end and returned at the other. He also wanted to build two footbridges. His application to the *Préfet* of the Eure informs us of his intentions, while a letter to Alice (written from Rouen) tells of the obstacles he was encountering at the Préfecture and on the part of certain villagers.

The matter was finally settled, and Monet went to see the director of the botanical gardens of Rouen, who gave him seedlings and plant bulbs; he bought others and sent the lot to Giverny, along with plenty of advice.

Another letter to the *Préfet* of the Eure is important, because in it he states for the first time that his pond was "for the pleasure of the eye and also for motifs to paint" (see p. 119), which contradicts the idea put forth by many critics that Monet, at least initially, had no such thing in mind. Henceforth, the garden and the pond were to be his constant preoccupation; when he left on trips, his letters home were always filled with suggestions.

The subsequent expansions and modifications are not always easy to date with much precision, despite the existence of survey maps and photographs, most of which can be found in Wildenstein's book (vol. III, 1979) and in the catalogues of the New York (1978) and the Paris (1983) exhibitions. In 1895, he paid the township the sum of 5,500 francs so that a piece of marshland would not be sold and drained. It was probably in 1897 that, just a few meters from the house, the West building was built, with a ground floor for the gardeners (there were sometimes as many as five), which was later turned into a garage and a darkroom, for Monet was very interested in photography. In 1901, he bought another piece of land and was able to expand the pond. In 1904, he added a trellis to the Japanese footbridge to grow wisteria. In 1910, he modified the contour of the pond's banks, and in 1914 he decided to built the great East studio where he was to paint the *Nymphéas*.

All in all, Monet spent more than forty years of his life at Giverny. The letters written during his absences, which were rather long at first, then more infrequent and of shorter duration, attest to his unfailing and conscientious interest in his garden.

He shared his passion with his friend, the painter Caillebotte, and with Octave Mirbeau, about whom he wrote to G. Geffroy: "Mirbeau has become a master gardener, he thinks of nothing else" (Letter of Oct. 7, 1890, catal. Librairie de l'Abbaye, 1982, no. 192). Mirbeau, on his end, wrote him (date unmentioned): "I am glad that

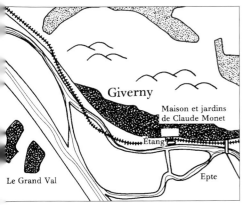

Map of Giverny

you are bringing Caillebotte, we shall talk about gardens. Art and literature are nonsense; the soil is the only thing that matters." (Quoted by C. Joyes, 1975, p. 19). Monet also became friends with Abbot Toussaint, the priest of Giverny, with whom he liked to discuss botany. Renoir at Cagnes, or Cézanne at Aix, never manifested a comparable passion for gardening.

As the opportunities presented themselves, Monet expanded his property until the limits which it still has today. For all of these reasons, and because a garden is a changing thing, it is important to take specific dates into account when one is speaking of Giverny. Moreover, the choice of flowers obviously followed the seasons: "Starting in the spring, we would change this carpet every two weeks, creating a new tableau each time in this space." (L. Gillet, *Le Gaulois*, Dec. 6, 1926). And yet it is never easy to determine the date of a given modification, the photographs and documents notwithstanding. In any event, it seems that, apart from an expansion around 1901, the water-lily pond itself was not the object of many transformations; thus, the admirably reconstituted garden which we can see today corresponds closely to the aspect it had during the last ten years of Monet's life.

The expense involved in the care and upkeep of these gardens obviously necessitated corresponding means. Monet had indeed lived in misery for a long time, but his situation improved little by little, such that by the 1890s his work was sell-

Plan of the gardens

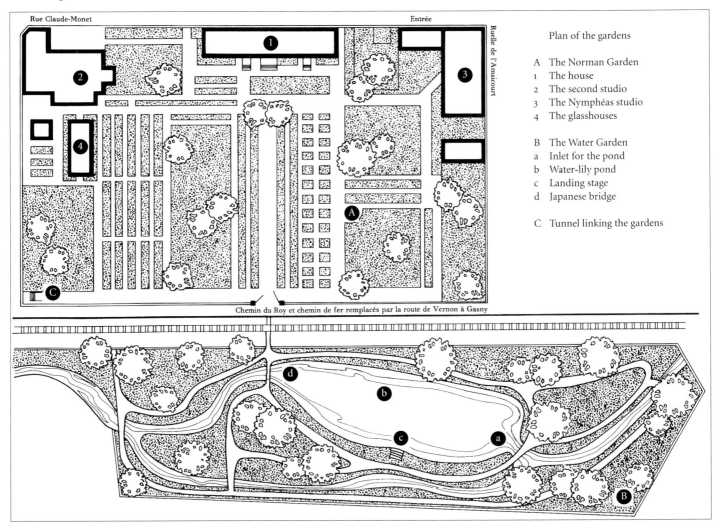

Plan of the gardens

A The Norman Garden
1 The house
2 The second studio
3 The Nymphéas studio
4 The glasshouses

B The Water Garden
a Inlet for the pond
b Water-lily pond
c Landing stage
d Japanese bridge

C Tunnel linking the gardens

ing well; he carefully managed the art market and consistently refused to give Durand-Ruel the monopoly of his production. Apart from his house, his garden, and his hired help, his only luxuries were his table and his automobile (he bought his first one in 1900). Monet was a great fan of automobile races and would often travel to see them.

Monet liked to receive guests in his house, which he decorated with an exquisite and original taste that contrasted with that of his contemporaries (when one considers the hideous furnishings of Zola, or Cézanne's indifference to his immediate surroundings). The dining-room painted in two shades of yellow, with matching Haviland porcelain tableware (probably chosen by Monet himself), was the scene of many a cordial meal; as for the fare, its quality was a legend in itself.

In order to have an idea or to begin to understand how Monet arrived at the major and unprecedented innovation of the *Nymphéas* series, one must first consult scattered and contradictory accounts. On this material, however, depends the answer to an important question: was the Monet of Giverny withdrawn into himself, and into his garden—that other self—or was he open to the world around him, especially at a time when ideas and the arts were changing at a rapid pace? Did he receive from the "outside world" any stimuli that could have guided his own work?

It has become customary to stereotype Monet as a rather hermitlike person who fled the city, avoided company, and found his happiness only in the intimate circle of his family and a few close friends. His avowed passion for his garden notwithstanding, this man whom some have called a homebody was very often away from Giverny: he travelled to Norway in 1895, to London several times between 1899 and 1904, to Madrid in 1904—a trip unknown before the recent publication of several letters by M. Guillaud—to Venice in 1908, not to mention short excursions in his automobile.

Precise information on his trips into Paris itself is relatively scarce. In 1921, he told Marcel Pays ("Une visite à Claude Monet", *Excelsior*, Jan. 26, 1921) that he had "not set foot in Paris in four years". But Geffroy, who tended to accentuate Monet's antisocial side, wrote that "during the years before the war and during the war, [they] fairly regularly attended the luncheons of the Académie Goncourt". More detailed information on this question is given by J.-P. Hoschédé, whose reminiscences often help to nuance Monet's traditional image: "If Monet willingly acquiesced to taking walks and making outings to satisfy the wishes of his children or of the whole family, he was also not averse to granting himself the pleasure of a few distractions when he went to Paris, always in the company of my mother. They would attend the premières of Mirbeau's plays, such as *Les Mauvais Bergers*, or *Les Affaires Sont les Affaires*, or a popular play such as *Chanteclair* or go to hear Chaliapin, see Pavlova or Loïe Fuller dance, or the Javanese dancers. They also liked to go the Théâtre Antoine." (1960, p. 88).

The legend of a Claude Monet who lived the life of a recluse at Giverny must be put to rest. It was due to Gustave Geffroy, who wrote such passages as: "And so Monet became entrenched in his love of solitude, his wildness, and his life withdrawn among flowers." ("Claude Monet", *L'Art et les artistes*, 1920). Others, such as Georges Grappe or Marcel Pays, may have harped on the difficulty of obtaining a meeting to lend more importance to their own accounts. It is true that around 1895, with Giverny having been more or less invaded by young American painters, Monet had to keep at bay importunate visitors desirous of receiving "lessons" from him; he made exceptions, however, for Robinson, Beckwith, Th. Butler and the Perrys, with whom he became friends. Finally, it should not be forgotten that Monet lived at Giverny for forty-three years and that it was only normal that, being a celebrity

Claude Monet
in front of the water-lily pond

and growing old, he should want to safeguard his creative work and his personal comfort. It should also be kept in mind that many visitors left no trace of their passage. Monet may have had a need for tranquility, but he never stopped receiving the frequent visits of certain intimates, the closest of which were Geffroy, Clemenceau, Mirbeau, Durand-Ruel, and the Bernheim brothers. Geffroy himself reports that he often went accompanied by friends or acquaintances, and he mentions in particular the engraver Victor Focillon (the father of Henri Focillon), Eugène Carrière, Maurice Hamel, Paul Clemenceau (the brother of the statesman), the writer Jean Ajalbert, Dr. Vaquez, a friend of the Nabis, Paul Gallimard, André Barbier, Georges Crès (the publisher), and added: "The Académie Goncourt was received [at Giverny] in the persons of Rosny senior, Léon Hennique, Lucien Descaves, Paul Margueritte, Octave Mirbeau", and Gustave Geffroy himself (1924, II chap. 36).

The list of the visitors to Giverny is finally a long one indeed; we have provided a chronological one (necessarily incomplete) at the end of this chapter (p. 18).

A break appears around the years 1896-1900. Before then, the best-known visitors were artists: Sargent, Berthe Morisot, Jacques-Emile Blanche, Cézanne, Rodin, Renoir… Monet kept actively in touch, at Giverny as well as in Paris, with his old friends of the Impressionist group and with other artists. We know that in 1895, he attended a banquet held in Paris in honor of Puvis de Chavannes's seventieth birthday.

Nymphéas,
Le Havre,
Musée des Beaux-Arts
André Malraux

View of the water-lily pond, circa 1925   Actual state

Starting at the turn of the century, though, it seems that the majority of his visitors were writers and critics. Monet was regularly in touch not only with his friend and confidant Gustave Geffroy, but also with the other members of the Académie Goncourt, and these were followed by other figures of the literary scene: Louis Vauxcelles, Louis Gillet, Paul Valéry (several times), Georges Grappe, Sacha Guitry. Finally, after 1914, the aging Monet left Giverny more infrequently and became more reluctant to receive. In 1914 or 1915, Clemenceau brought the Minister of Trade, Etienne Clémentel, to see him. A cultured man of taste and amateur painter, Clémentel was on friendly terms with Rodin and played a decisive role in the negotiations that led to Rodin's donation to the French State and the creation of the Musée Rodin. Monet got on well with the Minister, whom he visited several times at his home in Versailles. Clémentel rendered Monet various services and had the lucky idea of taking a colour photograph of him in front of the Nymphéas (see pp. 8-9).

If the list includes a large number of writers and journalists, it is probably because they left a record of their passage; we may assume that artists, dealers, and collectors probably made the trip to Giverny in comparable numbers. Monet was always willing to receive writers, even obscure ones (Valéry and Louis Gillet were hardly famous at the time of their first visit). Was he attempting to polish his "public relations" and shape an image of himself for posterity? Perhaps. He probably also profited from these meetings to pick up the latest art and literary news.

Monet may have known about Fauvism, which burst on the scene in 1905, the Ballets Russes of Sergey Diaghilev, Cubism, the beginnings of Abstraction. It is not unreasonable to think that on some trip to Paris, he may have seen the works of the rising generation of artists, many of whom proclaimed their admiration for him. Even if he did not regularly visit the Salon des Indépendants (to Louis

Vauxcelles he spoke of the "young people of the Indépendants", *L'Art et les artistes*, Dec. 1905) or the Salon d'Automne (we know that he saw the one in 1906, letter of Alice to Germaine Saleron of Oct. 24, 1906, catalogue Paris, 1983, p. 281), he did go many times to the gallery of Bernheim-Jeune, who often exhibited Matisse. Could it be that none of his visitors ever talked to him about the new tendencies in painting, ever showed him any photographs, or drew his attention to his possible influence on the young painters? Men like Geffroy, Gillet, or the astute critic Louis Vauxcelles, who gave Fauvism and Cubism their name, not to mention the Bernheim brothers, were too involved in the artistic life of their time not to have kept Monet up to date. The opposite would seem more unlikely.

"We talk to him about Cubism, we mention Picasso's name… he shrugs his shoulders: 'I've seen reproductions in magazines. I don't care for it… I don't want to see it, it would make me angry.'" Narrated by Jacques Salomon, *Chez Monet avec Vuillard et Roussel*. "L'Œil", May 1971, no. 197, p. 24. It has become commonplace to see the Monet of the *Nymphéas* as a precursor of abstract painting (see p. 75). There is no doubt that the abstract painters knew Monet's work and that they were marked by it. But did Monet himself not have knowledge of the first Parisian abstractionists—Delaunay, Kupka, Picabia, and others—who exhibited at the Salons and whose works were reproduced, sometimes even in the newspapers?

To get a better idea of the creator of the *Nymphéas* and of the atmosphere in which this revolutionary work was created, there is another source which up to now has not been studied, Claude Monet's library. Geffroy mentions a few titles, in particular Delacroix's *Journal*. Louis Vauxcelles noted in his house: "A library; few books, but good ones." (*L'Art et les artistes*, Nov. 1905). Maurice Kahn provided more details (*Le Temps*, June 1, 1904): "The library before me had books by Flaubert, the Goncourts, Zola, Mirbeau, Jules Renard, the *Critique d'avant-garde* of T. Duret, and several volumes by foreign authors formerly published by the *Revue Blanche*." Marthe de Fels and J.-P. Hoschédé give us further indications. Monet liked to read and discuss his favorite authors. This library[2] was in fact much larger and more varied in its composition than these scattered indications would seem to indicate. It featured editions of the great classics and of contemporary authors, as well as magazines, in particular the *Revue Blanche* series. Finally, there is much evidence in his correspondence proving that Monet regularly read the newspapers.

Thus, the *Nymphéas* are anything but the product of the obsession of a solitary, antisocial, and uninformed old man. It is a work born of the efforts and meditations of a man who was at the height of his powers, and for whom the practice of painting was accompanied by balanced intellectual pursuits, a reflection on his art, and lastly, a constant and focused interest in nature and flowers.

2. Its contents are being studied in more detail and will be presented in a separate publication [The project seems to be in abeyance (2006)].

List of Visitors to Giverny (abridged)

Date of first visit

Habitual visitors:
Georges Clemenceau, Gustave Geffroy, Paul and Georges Durand-Ruel, Gaston and Josse Bernheim, Octave Mirbeau

1885-1886
Auguste Renoir, Camille Pissarro, Alfred Sisley

1887
John Sargent, Théodore Robinson, Willard Leroy Metcalf, Gustave Caillebotte, Paul Signac, Thadée Natanson, Louis Anquetin

1889
Mr. and Mrs. Perry, Theo Van Gogh

1890
Berthe Morisot, Stephane Mallarmé

1893
Jacques-Emile Blanche

1894
Paul Cézanne, accompanied by Auguste Rodin and Auguste Renoir

1896
Isaac de Camondo

1898
Maurice Guillemot

1900
Lucien Guitry, Anatole France

1903
Paul Helleu, Étienne Moreau-Nélaton

1904
Maurice Kahn

1905
Louis Vauxcelles with Felix Borchardt, a German painter

1907
Louis Gillet

1908
Paul Valéry

Around 1910
Lucien Descaves and Léon Hennique, Pierre Bonnard

1914
Madame Cathelineau, Fernand Léger

1914-1915
Étienne Clémentel

1918
René Gimpel, Sacha Guitry

1919
Lucien Pissarro

1920
Kójiró Matsukata, Édouard Mortier the duc de Trévise, Maximilien Luce, Sadao Kuroki, Martin A. Ryerson, Arsène Alexandre

1921
Marcel Pays

1923
George Moore

Date unknown
Jean Ajalbert, André Barbier, Eugène Carrière, Georges Crès, Victor Focillon, Michel Georges-Michel, Maurice Hamel, Paul Margueritte, Ker-Xavier Roussel, François Thiebault-Sisson, Dr. Vaquez, Édouard Vuillard

Monet, Clemenceau, and Lily Butler
on the Japanese footbridge, June 1921

The Series of Water-Lilies

The Water Lilies[1] constitute a *series*, a giant series of over two hundred and fifty canvases. In fact, Monet is the inventor of the very principle of a series. As Georges Clemenceau humorously described the process: "We loaded the wheelbarrows, and sometimes even a small farm cart, with piles of equipment, so as to set up a row of outdoor studios, the easels being lined up on the grass for the battle between Monet and the sun. It was a very simple idea, but it had never been tried by any of the great painters. Monet can claim credit for it." (*op. cit.* 1928, p. 78).

There is no lack of eyewitness accounts of this practice. One of the oldest and least-known is that of Maurice Guillemot from 1898: "The peasant, a garden-helper who accompanied him, undid the packets—which is the word for stretched canvas put in pairs and numbered—and the artist set down to work. Fourteen paintings were started at the same time, almost like a scale of studies, depicting a single motif that varied according to the effects of the time of day, the sun-

light, and the clouds." ("Claude Monet", *La Revue Illustrée*, March 15, 1898, unpaginated).

This painter who has always been described, and who let himself be described not without some complacency, as a charming improviser who rebelled against all theoretical discourse, was in fact an artist for whom a deliberate and original intention always preceded an execution that was anything but spontaneous.

As early as the years between 1870-1880, Monet represented the same sites several times, varying only the light; this was the case for certain views of Argenteuil, and especially of the Gare Saint-Lazare. The idea of a series having been formulated, it was applied in an irregular fashion over the new few years. As did Cézanne who, on May 20, 1881, wrote to Zola, "I've started several studies in grey and sunny weather." Neither centring nor standpoint varied in his 1881-1885 *Views of L'Estaque*, or in certain *Mount Sainte-Victoire* canvases and the views of *Black Castle*; their only difference being in the play of colour, they effectively formed *series*.

According to numerous accounts, especially those of Clemenceau and Geffroy, and even of Monet himself as reported by the duc de Trévise[2], the procedure took on a completely systematic character: at first, Monet merely painted similar but distinct subjects (poplars); then he went on to representing the same subject, viewed from about the same spot (Haystacks, the Rouen Cathedral, Venice), setting up several easels and working on each canvas successively as the time of day changed the coloring of the motif.

Each theme had its own meaning, and from one series to the next there was an obvious progression, if certain criteria are taken into consideration: of all the trees, *poplars* are among the most flexible and mobile, they are the very model of an elegant and graceful form. And yet Victor Hugo said that "the poplar is the only tree which is dumb", which would not have much bearing on Monet's work were it not for the fact that this very quip is mentioned in the previously-cited article

1. The term *Nymphéas* will be used for the paintings in the Orangerie and "Water Lilies" for the series as a whole—Trans.

2. The duc de Trévise (1883-1946), a collector and art-lover who was open to the arts of all periods, was an outstanding figure in artistic circles and the founder of an association, *La Sauvegarde de l'art français*, which played an important role under his leadership. He visited Giverny in 1920 and wrote a very detailed account of his visit, but published it only after Monet's death. It has been quoted by most of the historians of the artist. On the other hand, an article by him (see bibliography), published just after his visit to Giverny, has scarcely been mentioned. A fellow-student of Monet's at Gleyre's studio, and an amateur painter all his life, the duc de Trévise wrote a particularly vivid account of the painter's work at Giverny. Contrary to certain affirmations, the duc de Trévise was never a member of the *Parlement* and he probably had no part in the negotiations concerning the *Nymphéas*. (On the duc de Trévise, see P. A. Lemoisne, *Bulletin de la Société de l'histoire de l'art français* (1947-1948), pp. 35-36, and Charles de Cossé Brissac, "Retour sur le passé, la présidence du duc de Trévise, 1921-1946", *Cahier de la Sauvegarde de l'art français*, no. 2, pp. 5-42).

on Monet by M. Guillemot. *Haystacks* also belong to the plant world, but they are the products of man's labor; they have a heavy, indefinite, and inelegant form. Hugo, always a good spokesman for the collective Mind, describes those that surrounded Boaz (in the *Légende des Siècles*) as being like "heaps of ruins".

The Rouen Cathedral is in complete opposition to the themes of the poplars and the haystacks, which are natural, perishable, interchangeable, and insignificant. The Gothic cathedrals, on the other hand, are unchanging, unique, glorious, images of Beauty itself, masterpieces of sacred architecture, and they were at the forefront of artistic concerns at the time; consider, for example, the famous book *Cathedrals* written by Monet's friend Auguste Rodin.

As for the water lilies, plants which emerge miraculously from the water and that are rich in poetic significance (cf. p. 99), it was to them that Monet devoted his largest series: not some twenty works or so, but over two hundred and fifty of them, many of very large format.

The very first paintings of the water-lily pond are almost square in format, which was already a first breaking away from the usual canvas shapes, for the square format was not very common, especially for Impressionist landscapes. Monet sometimes even chose a circular format, and he was practically the only Impressionist painter to do so.

The paintings dated 1899 and 1900 constitute a fairly homogeneous series: in fact, S. Patin (catalogue, 1980, p. 324) suggests that, at least for this series, the dates 1899 and 1900 may have been inscribed on works from 1898. Be that as it may, most of the canvases bearing this date are more or less square in format and represent the part of the pond which is closest to the road, with the footbridge and the willow branches.

In 1901 and 1902, Monet worked mostly on views of London and Vétheuil. Several canvases bear the date 1903: most of them depict the full length of the pond, the border between the water and the trees becoming less distinct.

Between 1904 and 1906, there are about twenty *dated* canvases of the Water Lilies, most of them of a square or nearly-square format. Monet was devoting part

The Water-lily Pond,
Green Harmony, 1899
Paris, Musée d'Orsay

of his time to painting views of London. From 1907, there are some thirty canvases of various formats, several of them circular. There is more sky, and sometimes the banks, which would have given an indication of depth or space, are not even depicted. The flowers float freely in a transparent medium, as if weightless; the painter, or the spectator, is not specifically situated. It is impossible to determine the angle of the point of view in relation to the surface of the water: are the tangles of vegetation afloat in the air, or plunged in the depths?

Before the exhibition in 1909 at Durand-Ruel's gallery (which was visited by Marcel Proust, in the company of Mme. Straus[3]), Monet destroyed a certain number of canvases. Only one, prematurely sold to an American collector, J.F. Sutton (priv. coll., U.S.A.), remains to give an idea of those that were lost. Monet himself wrote to Durand-Ruel on April 27, 1907, saying: "I have sold one of these canvases to Mr. Sutton. I am the first to regret it, because if I still had it in my possession, I would destroy it, and in any case, I would not want to include it in the planned exhibition." (Quoted by Venturi, 1939). What characterizes this canvas (repro. exhibition catalogue, Paris, 1983, p.153), as opposed to the ones that were "saved", is precisely its legibility, its almost naturalistic aspect, with the bank and the reflection of the sky being clearly indicated, while in other canvases of the same period the banks are not represented and there are no clues as to the perspective.

The 1909 exhibition itself had a particularly strong impact. A few particularly aware critics, such as Arsène Alexandre, Roger Marx, or Louis Gillet, sensed its powerfully innovative character. It was after visiting this exhibition that Charles Péguy, informed by Louis Gillet, wrote on the Water Lilies—and on the creative method involved, whose importance he had guessed—one of his rare texts on painting. As for A. Alexandre, one of the most astute and open critics of his generation (he was one of the few French critics who took an interest in the Bauhaus), he noted the characteristics that were to be accentuated in the later works: "… Mr. Claude Monet painted the surface of his pond, in which water lilies grow in a Japanese-style garden. But he has painted the surface only, seen in perspective, and there is no horizon in the picture, which has no beginning or end other than in

3. Mme. Emile Straus, the widow of the musician Georges Bizet and remarried to a lawyer, held a famous *salon* in Paris. Marcel Proust, who became her friend, was inspired by her in his portrayal of certain traits of the characters of Odette and the duchesse de Guermantes.

Water Lilies, 1907,
Saint-Etienne,
Musée d'Art et d'Industrie

the limits of the frame, such that the imagination is at leisure to prolong it at will. The only elements of the picture, therefore, are the watery mirror, the leaves and flowers which rest upon it, and then the infinitely varied and draped reflections of the surrounding landscape and of the sky above. In a word, they are paintings of reflections mixed with actual objects, but harmonized with them in a marvellous and capricious diversity. The most unexpected and the most true effects are never to be found twice in this vast series, which counts no less than forty pictures." (La Vie artistique: "Les Nymphéas de Claude Monet", *Le Figaro*, May 7, 1909, p. 5).

At the same time as he was turning out these forerunners of the great compositions of the Orangerie, Monet painted pictures inspired by subjects from the part of the garden lying closer to the house, representing specific motifs (irises, tree branches, etc.) very clearly.

In any case, with few exceptions, after 1909 (the date of his last exhibition of the series of Water Lilies), precise dating is impossible; a few photographs, indications noted on a canvas stretcher, or the presence of a particular work in an exhibition, can sometimes permit us to fix a limit in time *ante quo* or *post quem*. The evidence overwhelmingly suggests that certain canvases were reworked at intervals of several months, and even of several years.

Monet, like many of the other Impressionists, had long cherished the dream of painting murals; in 1887, in a contest for a decoration for the Hôtel de Ville of Paris, Monet failed to obtain the project in spite of Rodin's support. As early as 1898, in the precious article which shows Monet's passionate interest in his garden ("the master has a passion for flowers, and he reads more catalogues and horticultural price-lists than articles by aesthetes"), Maurice Guillemot mentions a "decoration for which he has already begun to do studies, of large panels which he will show me later in his studio. One must imagine a *circular room* whose wall-space, *below* the baseboard, is to be entirely occupied by a horizon of water dotted with plant life, walls of a transparency tinged with some green here, some mauve there, the calm and silence of still waters reflecting the spreading vegetation." (*La Revue Illustrée*, March 15, 1898, unpaginated). Not just the general outline, but the very principles of the quite original installation in the Orangerie have already been set down here.

In 1914, Monet had a new studio, much larger than the previous one, built on the east side of his property. It was in this studio, and not at the edge of the pond, that nearly all of the large *Nymphéas* compositions were painted, as their size did not permit them to be transported outside easily. And so, independently of Monet's deeper motives and the internal coherence of his development, it was also for reasons of convenience that, in his later years, he restricted himself to the subjects that were close at hand: his garden and the water-lily pond.

Monet had two separate ideas in mind; the first one involved the fact that none of his series had been preserved in their entirety: Clemenceau had violently deplored this at the time of the exhibition of the *Cathedrals* in 1895[4]. The other idea, prior to the juxtaposition of the large canvases in his new studio, was to create a series for a fixed presentation in a given architectural setting.

In 1909, A. Alexandre, obviously reporting Monet's own words, spoke of a round room (*Comoedia*, May 8, 1909). Over the years, the accounts by visitors increased, but there are contradictions as to the number of panels and Monet's intentions; and the painter himself was too busy with his work to worry about keeping to a precise and preestablished plan. The large canvases were placed on moveable easels, and it is obvious that from one visit to the next, the canvases changed place within the studio. Which is why Thiebault-Sisson mentions twelve panels, and Gimpel thirty.

4. *La Justice*, May 20, 1895. Clemenceau was particularly fond of this text, which he also published in his *Le Grand Pan*, Paris, 1896, pp. 427-437, and in *Claude Monet, les Nymphéas*, Paris, 1928, pp. 81-91, with some editing.

The Willow Tree, circa 1918,
Paris, Musée Marmottan

Water Lilies,
Paris, Musée Marmottan

It was in the midst of the enthusiasm of the armistice of November 11, 1918, that the idea of a gift to the State was born. No later than the 12th, Monet wrote to Clemenceau:

"Dear and Great Friend,
  I am just about to finish two decorative panels which I want to sign with the date of the Victory, and am asking you to offer them to the State by your intermediary.
  It is not very much, but it is the only way I have of taking part in the Victory. I would like these two panels to be placed in the Musée des Arts Décoratifs and would be pleased if if they could be chosen by you.
  I admire and embrace you with all my heart,
  Claude Monet

In response to this letter, Clemenceau, whom one would imagine had other things on his mind, devoted his first day of relaxation after the signature of the Armistice, on November 18, to a visit to Giverny. It should be noted that Monet speaks of only *two* panels and asks them to be placed in the Musée des Arts Décoratifs. This destination may have occurred to him because of the presence in this museum of the Moreau-Nélaton Donation[5], which included fourteen works by Monet. And then, he probably considered this museum more in relation to its role as antechamber to the Louvre than in terms of its specific vocation. This initial offer, to which Clemenceau enthusiastically gave his oral approval, was to be followed by a long, involved history, which is known to us only through incomplete and contradictory accounts, and which finally resulted in *eight* compositions consisting of twenty-two panels being installed in the Orangerie after Monet's death.

5. This important donation made to the Musées Nationaux in 1906 also included works by Corot, Manet, Fantin-Latour, Sisley, etc., and a rich collection of drawings.

The first project for a more or less elaborated installation dates from September 1920 and called for a special structure to be built in the garden of the Musée Rodin, along the rue de Varenne. R. Gordon published the plans and elevation. While the interior layout seemed relatively skilful and in accordance with Monet's intent, the outer appearance was heavy and inelegant. At the time, *thirteen* panels were involved. The board of the Musée Rodin, after deliberating on the 2nd of October, 1920, agreed to the principle of this installation; and the minutes added: "Mr. Bonnier, the architect chosen specifically by Claude Monet, has been obliged, in the last few days, to go work things out with him." Shortly after this approval of the principle, another article by Thiebault-Sisson was published (*Le Temps*, Oct. 14, 1920) describing the project at the Musée Rodin: "In this construction, which will be in the shape of a rotunda, the twelve canvases will be placed on the wall end to end, so that the succession will give the eye the impression of a single canvas. The series will be separated by relatively narrow openings, to allow visitors to enter and leave, or will be placed symmetrically on either side of the entrance and exit. The glass roof will be high up enough to leave between the skylight and the canvases sufficient space for Mr. Claude Monet to place some decorative motifs here and there, above the intervals between the series. The artist even has the intention of decorating the vestibule of this rotunda with a rather large composition." Thiebault-Sisson emphasized Clemenceau's role, suggesting that the initiative had come from him and that afterwards, even though he was no longer *Président du Conseil,* he continued to act as intermediary between the State and the donor. This article contains many errors in detail, which infirm the value of its information. After losing his bid for the presidency of the Republic to P. Deschanel at the Congress of Versailles on January 16, 1920, Clemenceau ostensibly withdrew from public life. On the other hand, the prestige of the "Tiger" was such that it was not necessary for him to intervene to tend to the interests of Claude Monet, who was well-known as his friend and protégé. Most likely, there was a tendency to satisfy his wishes—if not to anticipate them—in obviously minor matters, in proportion to his successor's desire to change politics where more important issues were involved. The tenor of Thiebault-Sisson's article was taken up by other journalists. Thus, H. Verne, who in 1927, as director of the Musées Nationaux, was to receive the definitive donation of the *Nymphéas,* wrote: "… a small temple will be raised in the garden of the Hôtel de Biron, near the Musée Rodin. There, in the midst of twelve panels, we will have the illusion of being on the very isle of Giverny where Claude Monet transformed the white water lilies of his pond into visions of color. We will be able to follow through its symphonic variations this miracle ignored by those who do not know how to see, but which is revealed to us by the hand and the eye of the painter: the changing light on a small surface of water speckled with a few flowers." (*Le Monde Illustré,* Oct. 23, 1920). Jean Villemer further noted: "… he wants a special pavilion in the garden of the Hôtel de Biron, a circular room in which his canvases will be placed standing on the floor itself, in an uninterrupted series, such that the spectator in the middle of the room will think that he is on the island of the Japanese pond and will see all around him what he would see in the garden of Giverny." (*Le Gaulois,* Oct. 16, 1920).

Clemenceau himself was no doubt anticipating Monet's intentions, or pushing them to their paradoxical extreme, when, as Lucien Descaves reported, he "turned around in the studio [at Giverny], intoxicating himself with painting, and then cried out: *Parbleu!* The door is what bothers me! We should be able to arrive in the studio by an elevator that puts us right in the middle of it!" (*Paris Magazine,* August 25, 1920).

Opposite:
"Morning" (detail)

2nd Room, North Wall
"The Clouds"
Three adjoining panels, W. 425 each; i.e. total W. 1275.
Inv. 20100

*That great modern and contemporary artist
who painted twenty-seven or thirty-five times
his famous* Nénuphars; *or* Nymphéas.

CHARLES PÉGUY
(Clio)

"… *the work in which Monet liberated himself from all tradition,
but which already lacks his initial freshness, is presented more abundantly
and ends with two special rooms with panels by the master, made
'for eternity', representing water lilies on the pond of his estate at Giverny.
This results in a sort of misleading superiority, and there is no doubt
that the admirers of Monet who tolerated this have done a great disservice
to the master's memory.*

*To be sure, no one has the right to raise obstacles to the course of art.
Each artist has his own destiny and must follow it. But, all the same, even
for the uninitiated spectator who studies the complete work, more eloquent
at times, did the artist always follow a direct path, did he follow his very
own path, a goal that he had set for himself, or did he go astray at some
point and lose himself? Now, in Monet this error is particularly apparent
and it is painful to behold. The work as a whole even gives the impression
of a positive catastrophe. To have begun as he did, to have created
such pearls so early, to have displayed such rare taste, such a keen eye,
such mastery, only to finish his career with such failures, is that not
a catastrophic drama?*

*The 'Nymphéas' are of course not without qualities. Not everyone can do
as much; if we examine these 'smudged expanses' closely, we can see the
technical know-how and the sonority of Monet's palette. But just the same,
how empty it is, what an obvious misunderstanding, what a strange and
really pathetic climax to the career of the author of the 'Woman in
Green' and of the 'Luncheon in the Forest'! How unfortunate that the
exigencies of creative work obliged the artist to betray at such a time his
initial efforts, and what vanity lured Monet into these problems of
monumental decoration when he had absolutely no talent for it. And how
ironic that France, which watched lightheartedly as her glorious son's
most remarkable masterpieces were dispersed, has erected for his weakest
and largest works a whole temple, which, by the way, looks more like
the parlor-cabin of an ocean liner.*"

ALEXANDRE BENOIS
Alexandre Benois réfléchit
(written on the occasion of the Claude Monet exhibition
at the Orangerie in 1931)

R. Gordon and C. Stuckey have tried to reconstitute what the presentation at the Musée Rodin would have looked like: a circular room, panels standing man-high, topped by a frieze of wisteria vines. A painting in the Musée de Dreux (cf. p. 42) gives an idea of the effect.

The Musée Rodin project was quickly abandoned, however. An addition of this importance to the Hôtel de Biron grounds could not be made without running into opposition. Monet himself seemed somewhat dissatisfied. To limit expense, Bonnier's successive projects had gradually reduced the space available for the paintings. Monet may also not have appreciated being housed in a building that could be taken for a mere "annex" to the Musée Rodin. Besides, a more interesting solution had come up.

In 1921, the administration of the Beaux-Arts decided to assign to the *Direction des Musées Nationaux* (as it was then called) the two buildings overlooking the Place de la Concorde, the Jeu de Paume, and the Orangerie, which until then had been used for their original purpose. The Orangerie became an annex of the Musée du Luxembourg, unanimously criticized for being too small, while the Jeu de Paume was to be used for temporary exhibitions and to house contemporary foreign painting.

Had the Administration deemed it more coherent and less costly to house the *Nymphéas* in an existing building and one which was to be devoted in part to living artists? Clemenceau visited the Orangerie and the Jeu de Paume on March 31, 1921, just after returning from a long and successful trip to the Orient and India, and advised Monet to accept the new proposition:

Paris, March 31, 1921

My Dear Friend,

I went this morning to visit the Jeu de Paume with Paul Léon, Geffroy, Bonnier. Good light which we can increase as needed by piercing the ceiling. Perhaps insufficient width, 11 m. We had a look at the Orangerie (by the river). 13 m 50 that seems very good to me. We will redo the ceiling as you wish. This will cost more than the Jeu de Paume, but Paul Leon is taking care of it. I advise you to shake on it. You should come to Paris before to see for yourself. Say when. I'll be there with the others.

I am delaying my trip to Vendee because of a little cough.

See you soon. Hurry up, for the works at the Orangerie will take a little longer than at the Jeu de Paume.

Yours always.

G. Clemenceau

There is a slight error in Clemenceau's figures, because the Orangerie and the Jeu de Paume have the same width (10 m). But he may have been talking about the length.

Monet, who was taken through the Jeu de Paume and the Orangerie in April 1921, was probably pleased, after some reticence, by the prospect of a larger space than that envisioned at the Musée Rodin and by such a prestigious location. When he went to see the Jeu de Paume installation, Monet visited the Dutch exhibition (probably the last painting exhibition that he ever saw) at which Bergotte, in one of the most famous passages of *A la recherche du temps perdu*, admired the "little yellow wall" in Vermeer's *View of Delft*, a further "encounter" between Proust and Monet which seems to have escaped notice until now.

It is difficult to follow the negotiations which took place in 1921. The few documents known (letters or newspaper articles) collected by D. Wildenstein are not

Wisteria,
Dreux,
Musée d'Art et d'Histoire
Marcel-Dessal

always easy to interpret and must be placed back into context. One must keep in mind Clemenceau's fall from political grace, Monet's difficult character, which was aggravated by age and the beginnings of a cataract condition, and the fact that his work was still not fully accepted by the majority of public opinion. Monet's idea of a circular painting that would surround the visitor may have sprung from the panoramic views popular in Paris at the end of the century. What poetic justice to install his *Nymphéas* in the very place that, in 1889, had housed the masterpiece of illustrative and narrative painting, *History of the Century,* a panorama by Stevens and Gervex! Be that as it may, the principle of the installation of a gift by Claude Monet to the French State in a building on the Place de la Concorde was accepted by all concerned.

Basing themselves on these scattered elements, certain historians have dramatized the situation, accusing the Administration of exacerbating the problems, and portraying a discouraged Monet, ready to renounce his gift. No conclusions can be drawn from the conversations more or less faithfully transcribed by journalists unfavorable to the incumbent government. For instance, what shows through in Marcel Pays's interview of G. Geffroy (*L'Excelsior,* May 16, 1921), is more the latter's ill-humor at the disgrace of his patron, Clemenceau, than Monet's. As for the frequently-cited letter from Monet to Durand-Ruel dated April 21, 1921, it has often been interpreted in this vein: "… I am having problems at the moment with the administration of the Beaux-Arts over my gift. Things are not going smoothly and—strictly between the two of us—it is getting on my nerves, and it keeps me from working." (The full text in Venturi, 1939, I, pp. 457-458). It would take never having negotiated a donation with an old man unfamiliar with legal constraints to deduce from this that Monet was about to consider withdrawing his gift.

Charles Stuckey invokes another letter from Monet to Georges Durand-Ruel (May 28, 1921), previously unpublished, but it makes no allusion, however indirect, either to the *Nymphéas* or to the Orangerie (see p. 119).

Two letters of Clemenceau dated November 2, 1921, one to Monet, and the other to Geffroy, prove that an agreement in principle had been reached, that Clemenceau's influence had been decisive, and that Geffroy had also intervened (see p. 120).

The Garden at Giverny,
circa 1918
Grenoble, Musée de Peinture
et de Sculpture

Other previously unpublished letters from Clemenceau to Monet (see p. 120) confirm that the obstacles had been removed. The architect Bonnier, the author of the Musée Rodin project, was passed over—to Monet's satisfaction, and perhaps even at his request—in favor of Camille Lefèvre, the head architect at the Louvre, who later very tastefully realized the artist's ideas.

Monet had always been hard to deal with and intractable in business matters. He once even managed to obtain a "moral reparation" from the State for its official refusals of the past by selling for a very high price (200,000 F) the *Women in a Garden* of 1866-1867, which entered the Luxembourg on April 7, 1921.

For the Administration to put at his disposal part of the Jeu de Paume or of the Orangerie was a much more generous proposal, and indeed a more flattering one, than the project for a construction in the garden of the Musée Rodin. The letter of November 22, 1921, to Joseph Durand-Ruel betrayed no regret: "The gift of my decoration to the State now being a fact (…) the space will be ready in the spring. I have only just enough time to finish up the work." (Venturi, I, p. 459). But according to Stuckey, "As it happened, Monet was unable to devote himself entirely to putting his decorations into shape, for he had new problems from the Ministry to deal with." This affirmation seems quite excessive: it was only normal that Monet, after the agreement on principle of November 1921, should have concentrated on the completion of his panels for the Orangerie, and that the working out of the architectural scheme should have entailed deliberations.

Here is an example of the kind of misunderstanding that took place, and that each time Clemenceau had to smooth out: in March 1922, just before the signing of the deed of donation, Monet wrote to Paul Léon, the director of the Beaux-Arts, and obtained no reply. He turned to Clemenceau, complaining that "I have committed myself, but not he, and the way things are going, I am afraid that not much will come of it. The Beaux-Arts are overburdened, without funds, and are only trying to stall for time." (Quoted by J. Martet, p. 67). Clemenceau's reply was masterful; but underneath the jocular tone may be sensed his firmness and irritation:

Paris, March 13, 1922

Dear Friend,

When I received your missive, I told myself: "Well, he must have sat down and got a nail stuck in his behind." And from your letter I learn that that is just about what happened.

A little bit of balm for the soul, a cigarette, and, brush in hand, go back into the great workshop of glory.

Paul Léon was unable to come on Sunday because he had a meeting at Angers. He sent me your paper, which I returned to him this morning for modifications. I will tell you which ones. Two problems of pure form for which I proposed some solutions to him. In a few days I will ask you for a meeting between the three of us.

Poor blue angel! What blue she must have in her heart to compensate for the darkness [*bitume*] of Claude Monet.

I embrace you with all my heart.

Clemenceau

P.S. Take the nails off your chairs before sitting down on them.

On April 12, 1922, the notarized deed was signed by Monet (p. 125). It is a precious document, first of all because it gives us the titles of the panels chosen by Monet and the precise conditions for their presentation: a plan and elevation were in fact appended to the deed (see pp. 46 and 47). It also puts an end to all of the talk about reservations and changes of mind on both sides. The State was contracting a legal obligation vis à vis of Monet, but also a moral one in the eyes of public opinion. As for Monet, he was committing himself to a precise selection and to a well-defined installation. Had the dimensions and spaces at the Orangerie (much larger than those at the Musée Rodin) not completely suited him, he would have continued to negotiate, or would have dropped his plan for a gift. Besides, Monet wrote a letter to Clemenceau to announce the signing of the agreement, but the tenor of this letter is known to us only though Clemenceau's reply. Monet must have expressed doubts about his work, for Clemenceau had to tell him that "... You are perfectly ridiculous when you tell me that you have doubts about what you are giving. You know full well that you have reached the limits of what can be achieved by the power of the brush and of the mind. If you were not also driven by an unending search for the beyond, you would not be the creator of all of the masterpieces with which France will fortunately be able to adorn herself... (April 17, 1922, quoted by H. Adhémar, 1967).

Apart from the plan appended to the deed of donation, several plans for the installation at the Orangerie have been preserved. On the first of these, there is no mention either of Monet or of the *Nymphéas*, and their future emplacement is occupied by rectangular rooms. The oldest one mentioning Monet is dated January 14, 1922; the precision of its indications reflects the preliminary agreement that had been reached shortly before, in November 1921. Henceforth, all of the

Plan appended

	1st Room				2nd Room			
Date 1922	Jan. 14	Jan. 20	March 7	Actual	Jan. 14	Jan. 20	March 7	Actual
Number of panels	10	10	10	10	10	10	10	12
Number of compositions	4	4	7	4	4	4	3	4
Total length	42.50	42.50	49.50	39.87	39.50	39.50	42.50	50.96

Dimensions of panels

	1st Room	2nd Room
North Wall	12.71 m	12.74 m
South Wall	12.70 m	12.75 m
West Wall	5.99 m	8.47 m
East Wall	8.46 m	17.00 m

plans, although differing on several points, in particular the vestibule, were to feature two oval rooms.

For the first room, the disposition finally adopted was about the same as what had been originally planned (one of the panels is slightly shorter). The plan dated March 7, however, proposed a very different arrangement: the room is bigger and instead of being divided into four sections, the wall is divided into seven distinct compositions, which would obviously have disrupted the impression of a continuous environment. The two doors to the second room to the east were replaced by a single one in the axis. Does this mean that Monet, who was no doubt giving instructions to the architect Camille Lefèvre, at one point considered using compositions already painted in such a segmented way?

For the second room, there were no differences between the two plans of January. But in the March plan, its size is reduced and it has only one door: it would have presented only three compositions which covered three additional meters. The final disposition reverted to the plan with four compositions of January, but they covered a greater surface area.

In all, the plans of January called for 82 linear meters of compositions, that of March, 92 m., and today's presentation, 90 m.

It is difficult to determine precisely what was the nature and the extent of Monet's work on the *Nymphéas* of the Orangerie between the signing of the deed in April 1922 and his death on December 5, 1926. Was the program such as it may be seen today at the Orangerie established in 1922—or even before—with Monet having only to complete or add finishing touches to compositions which were already well on their way, all the while painting other Water Lilies, today dispersed? Or did he execute new works fitted to the dimensions of the walls of the Orangerie, and taking into account the plans approved by him? Or, lastly, did his heirs choose from among the works left in his studio the twenty-two canvases (although the agreement stipulated only nineteen) that were the best suited?

Indeed, it is difficult, if not impossible, to say if Monet, at the time of the signing of the deed, had finished, or even definitely established, his program. It seems probable that, having a certain number of pictures of the same height (2 m.) and of the same series in the works, Monet may not always have shown the same panels to his visitors as being destined for the Orangerie. No conclusive indications are to be gained in comparing the titles in the deed with those of the compositions in place at the Orangerie[6]. The four titles given for the first room: *The Clouds, Morning Green Reflections* (in the deed: *Reflections of Green Trees,* with the word "Trees" crossed out; a significant correction), and *Setting Sun,* correspond more or less to the four compositions in place, which lend themselves to such vague titles. Two of the titles for the second room (*Morning* and *Reflections of Trees*) do not seem very appropriate for any of the compositions, and the third (*The Three Willows),* the only precise one, corresponds to none of them, for in this room there are three compositions with *two* willow trees. Either these compositions were reworked, or else Monet, not having fully established his program, just gave titles at random in the donation agreement.

Contrary to what has often been reported, the Administration fulfilled its part of the bargain within a reasonable lapse of time. The funds were made available on August 17, 1922, work began in October and seems to have been finished in following year. At any rate, the rooms were ready long before Monet's death, for in 1927 it was necessary to clean the rooms which had been ready "for over two years" (letter

6. René Huyghe says that, when they were installed in 1927, the lighter-toned paintings were grouped in the first room, and the darker ones in the second room.

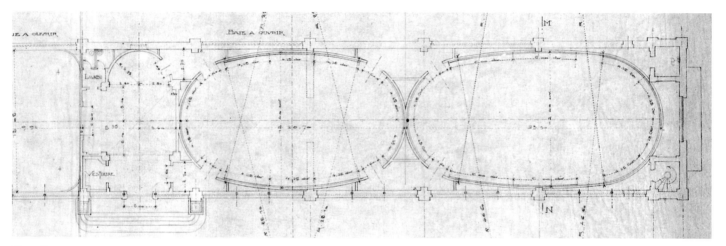

Plan of January 14, 1922

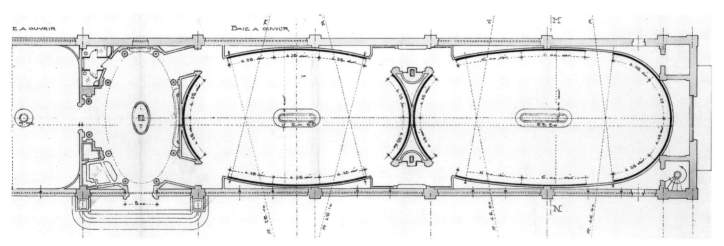

Plan of January 20, 1922

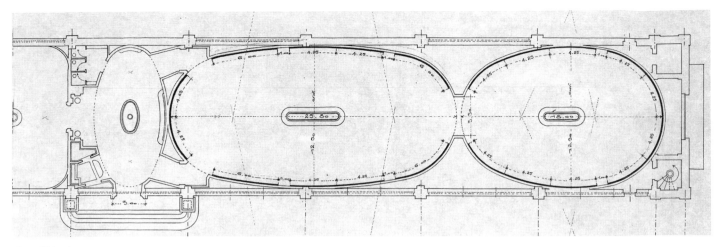

Plan of March 7, 1922

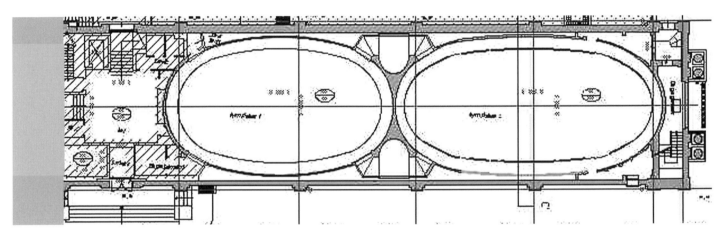

Plan altered during remodeling of the Orangerie (1965)

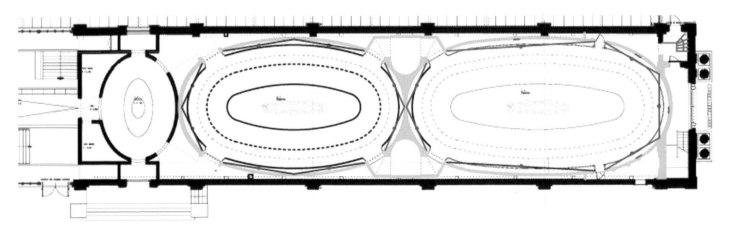

Final installation

47

Room 1, West Wall
"Setting Sun"
A panel, W. 600
Inv. 20103

from the head architect, May 7, 1927). It is only normal that Monet, aging and in a hurry to finish, may have found the Administration slow at first. Subsequently, however, the tables turned for several reasons: Monet's health, surprisingly good until then, began to fail; he became ill every winter. But most of all, because of the development of a cataract condition[7], his last years were plagued by increasing scruples. The first symptoms appeared before the war. During the war, he swung between periods of intense activity and fits of discouragement, due as much to current events as to his failing sight. Thus, he wrote to J.-P. Hoschedé on February 8, 1916: "I am caught up in my infernal work, as soon as I get up, I rush to the large studio. I leave it to have lunch and so on until the end of the day… in the evening I plunge into the newspapers." (Previously unpublished). But a few months later (Sept. 11): "I am doing fairly well, in spite of a few spells of discouragement, and then my confidence returns, but I am always afraid of not being able to see this enormous work through." (J. Martet, p. 64).

As early as 1919, Clemenceau, who was a trained physician, had recommended an operation. Monet feared it and wrote him: "As I told you in my telegram, I have given much thought to what you told me yesterday, it proves the friendship that you have for me, but, what can I say? I am very afraid that an operation would be the end of me, that once the bad eye has been eliminated, it will be the other's turn. And so I prefer making the most of my bad vision, even if it means giving up painting, but at least to see some of the things I love—the sky, the water, and the trees, not to mention those around me." (Nov. 10, 1919, J. Martet, p. 65).

In his correspondence with Minister Etienne Clémentel, whom he had taken into his confidence and who had facilitated the transport of the stretchers for the *Nymphéas* during the war, there are frequent allusions to his cataract; on December 19, 1920, in the midst of the negotiations, he wrote him: "I am in good health. Only my sight is weakening more and more, and this worries me." (P. Gassier, *Connaissance des arts*, April 1975, p. 96). This worry explains his haste to finalize the donation. It is true that in other letters, Monet informs his correspondent that there is an improvement and that his work is going well.

But it was especially after the signing of the deed of donation (April 12, 1922) that Monet's condition worsened and that his spirits took a plunge. It may be that he was traumatized by the two-year deadline that had been fixed. In his letters from the end of 1922, he complained of his sight and confessed his difficulties in finishing the *Nympheas:* "… All winter my door was closed to everyone. I felt that each day my sight was getting worse and I wanted to take advantage of what little of it remained to finish some of my decorations. And I was very mistaken in doing so. For I finally had to admit that I was only spoiling them, and that I was no longer able to do anything beautiful. And I destroyed several of my canvases. I am now nearly blind and have to give up doing any work. It is hard, but that's the way it is: a sad end, for all my good health!" (to Marc Elder, May 8, 1921, quoted by Marc Elder, p. 120)[8]. On September 8, he wrote Clemenceau: "Went to Paris yesterday for a consultation. Result: one eye completely gone, an operation necessary and even inevitable in the very near future. In the meantime, a treatment which could make the other eye better and allow me to paint. At the same time, I wanted to look in on the work at the Orangerie. Not a single workman. Complete silence. Just a small pile of debris at the door." J. Martet, p. 68). As we have already pointed out, the work began only a few weeks later.

An improvement permitted Monet to take up his brushes again. He underwent his first two operations in Paris in January 1923. His surgeon, Dr. Coutela, checked his progress in April; his recovery being slow, a third operation was necessary. Monet proved a difficult patient, but had a very strong constitution. In August he

7. On this subject there is an abundant bibliography based on medical analyses and numerous letters. Here we will mention briefly only those elements related to the completion of the *Nymphéas.*

8. In publishing this letter, Marc Elder made a few errors in transcription due to his difficulty in reading Monet's handwriting. Our thanks go to M.G. Fargeas, who consulted the original letters to Marc Elder and permitted us to correct these slight errors.

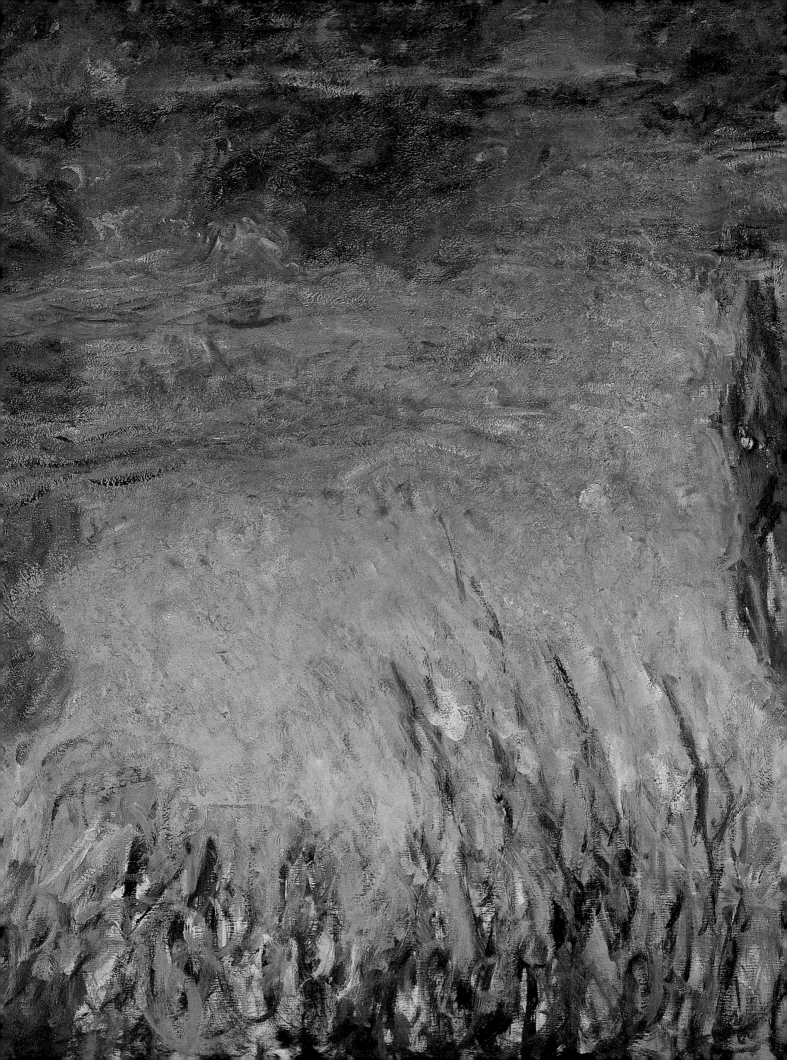

could read once more, though, as is frequent, his perception of colour had altered. His vision was affected by a yellowish cast which disappeared after a few months.

Periods of activity continued to alternate with spells of discouragement. On December 2, 1923, he wrote to Marc Elder: "I have gone back to work and haven't a moment to lose if the panels are to be ready in time." (Previously unpublished; see p. 121). And to the same correspondent, on February 25, 1924: "I must work without stop if I want to be ready to give my pictures to the State." (Previously unpublished; see p. 121). On March 6, 1924, to his old friend G. Geffroy: "The time is almost up for me to deliver the gift that I promised to the State. So these panels have to be finished and I am having a heck of a time and am completely upset, because I am far from being satisfied." (Previously unpublished). By comparing the dates of the letters (though not all of Monet's correspondence is known), it would seem as if he were playing a double game, expressing his discouragement to Clemenceau, yet declaring to his other correspondents his determination to work and to finish the panels for the Orangerie. As it was, Clemenceau ended up dropping the friendly and joking tone of his previous letters and reminded Monet of his commitments. The confrontation of these two old men, prepared to jeopardize their long-standing friendship over a common cause, is not without some pathos: "…each undertaking (Clemenceau reminds him) must have a beginning and an end. It was implicitly agreed that at a given time you would have an opinion, and it would seem from your letter that you don't have one. Is this any way to work things out?" (Published by A. Wormser, p. 26).

Monet turned a deaf ear and seemed prepared to renegue on his contract. The issue here was not the negligence of the Administration, but the painter's dissatisfaction. The stage was set for a power struggle between the two friends, which can be followed in the letters of Clemenceau from March 1, 1924, until the break of January 7, 1925, and their reconciliation in February 1925 (see p. 121-123).

In a long letter dated October 8, 1924 (see p. 122), Clemenceau summarized the problem both from the artistic and from the administrative points of view:

"First you wanted to finish the unfinished sections. It was not very necessary, but it was understandable. Then you had the absurd idea of improving the others. Who, better than you, knows that the impressions of a painter change all the time? If you went back with your canvases to the cathedral of Rouen, what would you not find to change? You made some new canvases, most of which were and still are masterpieces if you haven't spoiled them… at your request, a contract was drawn up between you and *France* in which the State has kept all of its commitments. You asked for the *postponement* of yours and, through my intervention, *it was granted…* On your account, the State is obliged to go to great expense, because of what you requested and even approved *in person*. You must therefore make an end of it artistically and honorably, for there are no *ifs* in the commitments which you have made."

In 1925, Monet confided to Dr. Mawas that he was like a man who was "completely discouraged, not to say finished" (letter of May 24, 1925; previously unpublished).

An important letter to Marc Elder (previously unpublished), dated October 16, 1925, attests to the change that had taken place in Monet's vision and also explains how he was finally able to bring the *Nymphéas* to completion: "You may already known that I have regained my true sight, which for me is like a new lease on life, and that I have gone back to work (see p. 124)."

After more than a year, Clemenceau finally won out, such that on February 8, 1926, he was able to write to Monet: "I was quite pleased to hear that the first shipment needed only for 'the paint *to dry*. And when you say that you are *very pleased*,

Blue Water Lilies,
Paris, Musée d'Orsay

Water Lilies, 1917,
Paris, Musée Marmottan

that means something." (see p. 124). And yet, Monet's hesitations were not finished, since on September 18, 1926, he stated: "Know that if I don't regain strength enough to do what I want to my panels, I have decided to give them as they are or at least part of them." (see p. 124). One wonders to what extent Clemenceau, to excuse his old friend, may have influenced or contrived the conversation during which Monet reportedly expressed his wish that the panels not be exhibited during his lifetime (G. Clemenceau, 1928, p. 38). According to J.-P. Hoschedé, Monet visited the Orangerie again in 1925 to see the rooms, "to give instructions and to indicate precisely the order in which the panels were to be placed." (1960, p. 15).

After Claude Monet's death on December 5, 1926, the installation was realized fairly rapidly; on January 31, 1927, the Laurent-Fournier establishment accepted the job of mounting the *Nymphéas* panels delivered separately, and an estimate dated February 25 gives a list which corresponds to what is in place today:

    19 panels of 2.00 x 4.30
    2 panels of 2.00 x 2.15
    1 panel of 2.00 x 6.00

There are traces of painting done at the borders between the panels, but no one knows by whom. On March 19, Blanche Hoschedé, the artist's stepdaughter, wrote back to Henri Verne, Director of the Musées Nationaux, inviting him to see the works in place on March 26. The inauguration was held on May 17. The day before, Clemenceau visited the museum which, without him, would never have come into existence. The long-awaited *Nymphéas* immediately inspired commentaries and the admiration of writers and critics, and attracted the interest of the public.

Francois Monod, the curator of the Musée du Luxembourg, to which the Orangerie was temporarily attached, gives a good idea of the general impression in a letter to Clemenceau: "The *Nymphéas* in our rooms at the Orangerie make a deep impression on visitors from all walks of life; they are all captivated, enchanted by this marvellous poem" (which he relates to the work of Walt Whitman). This sentence comes from a previously unpublished letter thanking Clemenceau for his book on the *Nymphéas,* which remains one of the most accurate accounts of Monet's intentions.

In it, Clemenceau complains of a "passive conspiracy of silence, unconsciously supported by administrative carelessness. At the terrace of the Tuileries, there is a small grey panel, not much larger than the bottom of my hat, which looks as if it were trying to tell the public that there is something there. Last month, just a few steps away, there was a gigantic sign superbly announcing a dog show. The public did not hesitate…" (Clemenceau, 1928, pp. 93-94).

The annual of the Musées Nationaux published in 1928 mentioned the opening of the Orangerie and commented on the *Nymphéas* as follows:

"In each of these series, [Monet] executed, after a given subject, a large number of paintings, all very different from one another. The difference between them is due to the fact that in each one the site is represented in a different season, at a different time of day, or in a different atmosphere. In other words, it is a demonstration of the fact that the atmosphere and natural light being infinitely variable, they give an infinite variety of aspects to a same subject.

The most extensive and the last of Claude Monet's series is that of the *Nymphéas.*

He began with studies of the pond in his garden at Giverny. It soon suggested to him vast symphonies which, year after year, took him further and further away from a merely objective study.

He had a vast studio built near the pond. The canvases were stretched on long, vertical supports similar to those used for drying in dyeing factories.

Claude Monet destroyed a large number of the decorations composed in this way.

He chose seventeen of them in which all the poetry of water, from daybreak to day's end, is expressed. Placed in the Musée de l'Orangerie with the help and under the supervision of his friend M. Georges Clemenceau, they represent the supreme blossoming of Impressionist art." It should be noted that seventeen, and not twenty-two, panels are mentioned; proof that they were not joined when they arrived.

In August 1944, during the battle for the Liberation of Paris, five shells fell on the rooms of the *Nymphéas;* two panels (those situated on the wall between the two rooms) were slightly damaged and immediately restored. In 1984, this restoration work was renewed and a general cleaning was effected.

Starting in 1958, the Musées Nationaux were enriched by the donation of a splendid collection of 19th and 20th-century paintings assembled by Paul Guillaume and then by his widow, the late Mrs. Jean Walter, who donated her collection with particularly generous conditions. At her request, they were placed in the Musée de l'Orangerie, which entailed the installation, in 1966, of artificial lighting in the rooms of the *Nymphéas.* In 1978, cracks were observed in the walls which, although they posed no threat to Monet's panels, weakened the structure of the building. Since it was impossible to remove the *Nymphéas,* the foundations of the building themselves were consolidated with micro-stakes. The lighting of Monet's rooms was redesigned so as to approximate outdoor lighting as closely as possible, in accordance with the artist's wishes; Mrs. Walter's collection was installed, after her death, in the remaining rooms of the Orangerie.

The Panels
of the
Orangerie

In their final state, the *Nymphéas* of the Orangerie comprise eight compositions divided between two rooms. The first impression—which no photograph can communicate—is one of awe and disorientation. Whether the visitor arrives from the rooms on the first floor—which, before the installation of the Walter-Guillaume Collections, housed the most diverse exhibitions, more often than not totally unrelated to Monet—or from the outside, leaving behind one of the most composed cityscapes in the world, the Place de la Concorde, the Tuileries, and the Seine, he steps into an entirely different realm.

There is an initial feeling of astonishment: it is not like being in a museum room in which a series of paintings has been displayed, or in an architecture which has been given a mural decoration. One is plunged in a colored environment, situated at eye-level, scarcely interrupted by two passageways, and occupying the entire visual field of an adult spectator looking straight ahead, neither raising nor lowering his gaze.

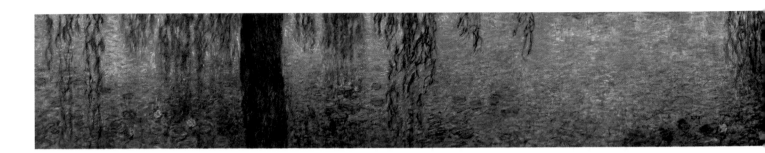

What reinforces this impression of it being a whole without a beginning or an end rather than a contrived succession, is the absence of definite details. There is nothing which catches the eye, no fragment calling attention to itself. One can barely distinguish here and there—and only by paying close attention—a drooping branch, flowers floating, and in the second room only, the trunks of willow trees.

The color-scheme is homogenous and not very varied, dominated by violet-blues and greens, highlighted by the bright spots of flowers. There is one exception, in the first panel of the first room, long streaks of red and yellow which suggest, but not insistently, the blaze of a setting sun. But, again, neither the flowers, nor the banks, nor even the willows, completely stop the eye. The gaze wanders in a circle, passing from one panel to the next, focusing only when one approaches for a closer look at the brushwork.

There is little or no "drawing" as such. Often, it is impossible to say if such and such a part of the canvas represents the surface of the water, the bottom of the pond seen in transparency, the grass on the banks, a branch, or a cloud. As for the water lilies, they appear only in four or five places: they are rarely placed in a clearly "stepped" way, neither their contours, which are scarcely indicated in perspective, nor their decreasing size, really help to suggest space.

A few critics of the twenties said that it was like being on the island in the garden and walking around it as one went around the room. But one could also imagine the opposite: that one is walking around the garden itself. Actually, representation has—once again—given us the slip. Monet is skirting the abstract here, not only because the representational details emerge here and there "in close-up" (C. Moffett) and then fade away, but above all because the general approach he adopted implies the refusal of literal representation. In Mondrian, the abstract painting is a wall; in Delaunay, it is a window or a mirror; in Lissitzky, a mechanism; in Kandinsky of 1912-1914, it is the quickening of the World. Kandinsky's large *Compositions* (V, VI, VII, etc.) which were preceded by paintings which he himself called *Impressions* (no mere coincidence), are of a large horizontal format close to that of the *Nymphéas*.

We know for a fact that seeing a *Haystack* by Monet had a decisive impact on Kandinsky (see p. 75); one must conclude that, whether he was in Paris or in Munich, Kandinsky kept informed about Monet's work. For the two artists, the abandonment of representation (with, in Monet's case, all due reserve) was not a sudden negation, but part of a coherent, and probably premeditated, endeavor; one which implied the search for a meaning. To stress the abstract quality of the *Nymphéas* does not detract from the work's significance, on the contrary. The cosmic resonance which their commentators, and Clemenceau first of all, detected very early, is perceptible only if one equally recognizes the innovative quality of the *Nymphéas* from a purely formal and material point of view. It is symptomatic, *a contrario*, that it was just those writers (A. Lhote, E. d'Ors…) who wanted to reduce them to a banal decorative function, who also proved to be insensitive to their poetic quality.

The coherence of Monet's endeavors also appears in the way he treated space and eliminated depth. The denial of Albertian perspective[1] by Monet was not just a matter of rejecting a tradition which he judged to be obsolete; he had enough experience with his craft and the art of the past to know that the representation of space in painting is not an innocent act. In the *Nymphéas,* the choice of a format corresponding to the totality of the visual field, the defocalization, the asymmetry, the absence of points of reference and contours, the absence of planes, suggest an immersion in a timeless chaos; just as, at the antipodes of the *Nymphéas*, in the *Virgin and Chancellor Rolin,* for example, the square format, the centered and strictly symmetrical composition, the clearly defined and hierarchical sequence of the planes, are not simply the description of a gratuitous setting, but the ordering of the sacred and profane microcosm around the Christ Child[2].

It goes without saying that this calling into question of Albertian space was not due solely to Monet. For four centuries, Western art had been ruled by a certain

1. According to the Quattrocento architect Leon Battista Alberti, the painting was considered as a section of the visual pyramid formed by the convergence of the light rays on the eye; a conception which governed pictorial practice until the 19th century.

2. These innovations can be related, as S. Levine has done, to the beginnings of the cinema. He also pointed out that the opening of the Orangerie was contemporary with Abel Gance's triple-screen (Stephen Z. Levine, "Monet, lumière, and cinematic time", in *The Journal of Aesthetics and Art Criticism,* Summer 1978, XXXVI, pp. 441-447). The patent for the triple-screen was issued on August 20, 1926, and the film *Napoléon* presented in Paris in April 1927.

Jan Van Eyck,
The Virigin and Chancellor Rolin,
Paris, Musée du Louvre

1st Room, East Wall
"Green Reflections"
Two adjoining panels, W. 425 each; i.e. total W. 1275
Inv. 20102

"*We can imagine a Claude Monet going towards the use of the great light and shimmering expanses that were the domain of Veronese or of Tiepolo. Let us imagine no more, and consider his supreme work, the* Nymphéas. *Despite their monumental size, they manifest none of the characteristics of the great Venetian or Flemish decorations. The disposition of his spirit seems to be that of a great "easel" painter who decides to give his vision a vast enough—a significant enough—field to encompass the world. (A mirror of water will suffice to identify oneself with the Universe). A cosmic vision, I would like to say, if this term had not been deviated so much in recent times and proffered in relation to just about anyone or anything. Thus Michelangelo, the creator of unique and solitary figures, waits for the day when a Vatican chapel will enable him to blossom, to show his omnipotence. Which is why it pleases me seriously to say of the Orangerie of the Tuileries that it is the Sistine Chapel of Impressionism. A deserted place in the heart of Paris, conferring, as it were, the consecration of the inaccessible to the great work which lies within: one of the summits of the French genius.*"

ANDRE MASSON
"Monet le fondateur", *Verve*, vol. VLI, nos. 27 and 28, p. 68

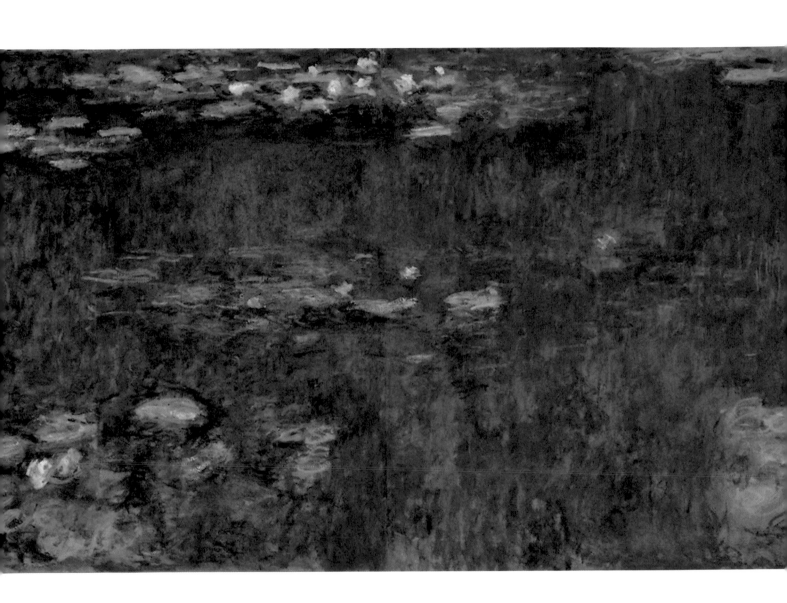

It's unimaginable—paintings so vast, so incommensurable,
were made in front of such a tiny pond.

RIOPELLE
(quoted by Jean-Dominique Rey,
"La dernière révolution: le spectateur,
partie intégrante de l'œuvre",
Galerie Jardin des Arts, July-Aug. 1974, p. 26)

Opposite:
"Tree Reflections" (detail)

2nd Room, West Wall
"Tree Reflections"
Two adjoining panels W. 425; i.e. total W. 850
Inv. 20107

The Nymphéas *of the Orangerie are a work that is entirely constructed, and the actual pond is no longer there as a model but as a master… We can see to what extent the painting of the late Monet was a thing of the mind [*"chose mentale"*]… the raising of the horizon… is now absolute, the sky or the distance appear only as an inversion, and the surface of the water rises toward the vertical all around us, which creates the illusion of flying or of diving.*

MICHEL BUTOR
Art de France, 1963, p. 297
© Éditions Hermann

number of principles for the representation of space and volume as defined by the artists and theoreticians of the Italian Renaissance. They began to be questioned, without fanfare, by Manet. Afterwards, the credit for this undertaking usually goes to Cézanne and Gauguin. Monet and the other Impressionists are rarely associated with this development; and yet, they too, along with all of the other progressive painters of the last quarter of the 19th century, abandoned Albertian space and strove to define another.

In quite a few works previous to the *Nymphéas,* Monet had had occasion to show his disinterest in or to deal lightly with conventional perspective. The *Poplars,* or certain *Barques* of 1885-1888, especially those in the Tokyo Museum of Occidental Art, display an almost complete absence of perspective: rising planes, little or no sky, carpet-like patterns. The influence of Japanese prints notwithstanding, the traditional conventions of representation were simply ignored here, more so, in fact, than abolished.

The large *Nymphéas* go even further in this direction. Volume and depth are completely absent. All of the pictorial elements have been placed on the same plane, devoid of thickness. Monet avoided any motif which could have suggested space: the water-lily flowers are generally depicted of fairly similar size, regardless of their position on the canvas, so as to avoid all suggestion of a stepwise progression in depth.

With the exception of a few paintings in which Monet, curiously enough, exaggerated traditional perspective effects by placing himself in the axis of the center path, his views of the garden are also devoid of perspective. The flowers are reduced to colored spots and the different species blend, in the same way that Monet mixed all kinds of flowers together in his garden. Ever faithful to his realist credo, Monet did not cheat with what he saw; his breaking away from linear perspective was also involved in his planning for and maintenance of the garden, as flowers of the same species could be of different sizes, they alone could not indicate scale or distance. The water-lily pond, especially, with its carefully designed irregular banks, never suggests receding distance as a rectilinear shape would. We are plunged into a substance which is both liquid and organic, and in which the light comes from nowhere. If we want to stick to a formalist analysis, as does André Lhote—who went astray in his interpretation of Monet anyway—we could at the very most remark on the multiplicity of the points of view, or, more exactly, on the different distances between the painter and his subject. All in all, Monet's approach is at the same time less rigid and more general than Gauguin's, and perhaps even than Cézanne's; although there is an obvious relationship between the *Nymphéas* and certain representations of the *Château Noir* or late works such as *Bibémus.*

This representation of an all-encompassing, open space, or rather one in which the painter and the spectator can roam about, should it not be related to the very disposition of the *Nymphéas* in the Orangerie? An easel painting, with its limited dimensions, cannot offer such an environment; but the disposition at the Orangerie requested by Monet guarantees it.

The *Haystacks* and *Cathedrals* series, deliberately painted as series and exhibited together, had already challenged the spectator in an unexpected way. In the past, an artist would, on the contrary, have hidden the execution of several similar versions of the same motif. Monet made it the very principle of the revelation of his method. In the Orangerie, it was the surrounding, the complete encirclement of the spectator – the witness – that Monet stubbornly sought, because in 1898, when the theme of the *Nymphéas* was still new to him, he was already talking of a circular space, and the original presentation achieved in the Orangerie gradually took shape over the years.

Monet in his studio at Giverny
in front of one of the *Nymphéas* panels
for the Orangerie (Room 1, South Wall)

Opposite:
"Morning" (detail)

Monet in his studio at Giverny

Opposite:
"Setting Sun" (detail)

This again brings up the question of the relation of Monet's work to that of his fellow artists at the time. The abolition of Renaissance perspective, the passion for mural decoration[1], the respect of the two-dimensional surface of the support, a new reflection on the problems of *representation*, all of these were concerns which Monet shared with many other artists. Moreover, Monet took an early interest in Japanese prints, at a time when they were just coming to the attention of Parisian art circles. It is highly probable that he saw a certain number of these prints during his trip to Holland in 1870. Later, when he had the means to do so, he collected them systematically and hung them on the walls of his house at Giverny. After a long period of neglect, this fine collection has been put back in place and its contents recently studied in detail[4].

Now, given this obvious interest and their daily presence in his home, can we deduce an actual "influence", at least on the *Nymphéas*? Before becoming a fashion in the last third of the century Japonism had been both a stimulus and an opportune argument for Western artists. Contrary to what is generally believed, the two-dimensional representational arts of Japan—the print being only one of the kinds of support—were known in the West long before 1850, but they were seen as belonging to a mode of representation that was completely foreign to Western art, and so were rejected as models. Delacroix mentioned them in his *Journal*, and there are allusions in the novels of the period also. A text on Eugène Devéria from 1826 which previously escaped attention was even more explicit[5].

The time was not yet ready, for the calling into question of Albertian space had not yet begun. With Delacroix and Courbet, it was barely touched upon. The vogue for Japanese prints around 1860 coincided with this questioning; and this was not fortuitous. Artists discovered that there was another mode of representation of space, just as coherent, but different from the one to which they had been accustomed. A similar process occurred forty years later with the discovery of "Negro" art. Subsequently, the Japoniste style became trivialized, and at the time of the painting of the *Nymphéas*, they were nothing more than a fashion, and a rather faded one at that.

It has been said that the vogue for Japan may even have inspired the design of the pool at Giverny. But, apart from the "Japanese footbridge", which can be considered as a passing allusion, and in spite of the precise knowledge that Monet may have had of the Japanese-style gardens then in fashion, it would seem to be less a matter of imitation here than of a similar spirit. Monet bypassed the various traditions in Western gardens in favor of an original conception which is not unrelated to that of the Japanese garden: the garden at Giverny is a closed world, separate from the surrounding landscape, and with constant treats for the eye; it changes as soon as one moves around; there is a multitude of points of view, but no special one in particular, and no deep perspective[6].

Monet in his old age, therefore, did not restrict himself to repeating formulas, or to exploiting the artistic feats of his early years. Like Cézanne and Degas, to mention only examples of his generation, he continued to seek—and to find. He was in no way behind the times vis à vis of the upcoming generation of painters, who were particularly inventive as it was. The *Nymphéas* and the pictorial language they involved brought to the expression of space and time a solution no less novel than that of Cubism or of Futurism; we will see in the next chapter the extent to which Monet counted, even after his death, in the development of Abstraction, even in its most recent forms.

3. In order not to lose sight of the great novelty of the *Nymphéas*, it should be remembered that Claude Monet, like all of his friends of the Impressionist group, not to mention the non-conformist artists of the late 19th century in general, and with the exception of a few early paintings, had been able to express himself only in small-format works. Being rejected by officialdom and public opinion, these artists never had the chance to do otherwise. The exceptions are rare: Gauguin and Manet had indeed given much thought to the "wall", which became one of the obsessions of the Nabis, but they received no commissions for murals in Paris. The decorations of Odilon Redon and of Bonnard were of a private character. In short, no profoundly innovative painter had been entrusted with a mural decoration in Paris since the Delacroix of the Chapelle des Saints-Anges at Saint-Sulpice.

4. G. Aïtken and M. Delafond, Paris, 1983.

5. "No Chinese fans or folding-screens, no Japanese boxes could give you a more grotesque idea of how to paint (…) It is generally thought (…) that there are rounded bodies and that they are unequally lit by the sun. M. Devéria does away with rounded bodies and so with the passage from light to shadow (…). The head, the legs, the arms are as flat as cookies." (Louis Vitet, *Compte rendu du Salon de 1826*.)

6. On this, see: John House, catalogue 1983, p. 152.

The Path to Abstraction

The majority of the articles published in great numbers at Monet's death (Dec. 5, 1926) emphasized his role as the creator of Impressionism, spoke with admiration of the paintings of the Argenteuil period, and remarked on an extraordinary visual acuity which accounted for his ever-increasing fondness for the most fleeting spectacles of nature and the most subtle color-schemes: ice floes breaking up, views of the Seine at Giverny, of the sea at Belle-Ile, and finally the series. In many articles, though, there is a touch of reserve, the author detecting in the *Nymphéas* a sort of weakening of Monet's "genius". It should be kept in mind, however, that most of the writers of the obituaries had not seen the great *Nymphéas* compositions yet, as the Orangerie did not open before May 17, 1927.

Claude Monet's decisive importance as an immediate precursor, even before 1914, on the path taken by the abstract painters was acknowledged, and with particular emphasis, by those directly concerned themselves. Their testimony has

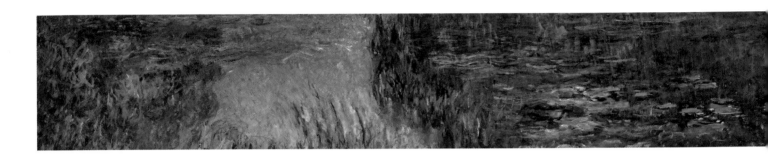

often remained unpublished, or else was little known in France at the time: the most important and the one least open to question is Kandinsky's. He tells how in looking at a *Haystack* by Monet—probably in the winter of 1896-1897 at the Kunsthaus in Zürich (D.W., n° 1288)[1]—he discovered the possibility of painting without representation. The text is worth quoting again:

"… I experienced two events which left their impression on me for the rest of my life and which affected me to the very depths of my being. These were an Impressionist exhibition in Moscow—above all a "Haystack" by Monet—and a performance of Wagner at the theater of the Court: Lohengrin… And suddenly, for the first time, I was seeing a painting… I felt confusedly that the painting had no object… All of this was very confusing for me, and I was unable to draw the elementary conclusions from this experience. But what was perfectly clear to me was the unsuspected power of the palette, which had remained hidden from me until then and which exceeded my wildest dreams. It gave force to the painting and a tremendous impact. But unconsciously too, the object as an indispensable element of the picture was discredited as a result."[2]

As for Malevich, he may have been light years away from Monet as a painter, but his importance as a theoretician of abstract art is indisputable, and he wrote: "Neither in the *Rouen Cathedral,* nor in the *Market* (by the painter Tarkhov)[3], do we see that the artist concerned himself with rendering the images of objects or of beings. The themes of the "cathedral" or of the "market" themselves are not so important, as against the pictorial relations, the changes of the colored elements. For most people, such paintings, with all of their changes, are not worth a thing because they do not depict the world in a concrete manner."[4] This refusal to read the Cathedrals in a "realist" way was rather courageous on Malevich's part, considering the date at which he was writing, 1929, for the official Soviet ideology condemned all forms of abstraction; nevertheless, he emphasized that: "It is not possible to say

1. See M. Hoog, *Revue du Louvre*, 1981, p. 22.

2. *Rückblicke*, Berlin, 1913.

3. The Russian painter Tarkhov (1871-1830) came to Paris early in his career, was marked by Impressionism, then gravitated towards Fauvism, and came to the attention of Vollard in particular. There is precisely a market scene reproduced in M.A. Leblond's study of Tarkhov (*Peintres de Race*, Paris, 1910, pp. 81-97).

4. Malevich, "L'Esthétique", *Nova Gueneratsiya* (New Generation), no. 12, Kharkov, 1929, p. 68. The French translation of this text (from which the English translation was realized) was provided to us by V. and J.-C. Marcadé, whom we take this opportunity to thank.

Opposite:
Clear Morning with Willows (detail)

that Claude Monet, in the *Rouen Cathedral,* reflected bourgeois religious ideology. This is because Monet was working above all on changes in the purely physical aspect of light." We could have quoted other texts in the same vein, by Larionov or Delaunay, supporting their position more often with the *Haystacks* or the *Rouen Cathedral* than with the *Nymphéas,* it is true, but the coherence of Monet's efforts is such that these texts may justifiably be applied to his work as a whole. In the case of Malevich, who hardly left the Soviet Union, it is only normal that he does not mention the *Nymphéas.* The rejection of the anecdotal by the Impressionists, which became little by little a rejection of all representation, found its culmination in the *Nymphéas,* no less than in the first abstract paintings of Kandinsky, Kupka, Larionov, or Delaunay, and especially in the last two, who were led to abstraction through the study of light.

As proof *a contrario,* there is the incomprehension of André Lhote, which was significant of the attitude of Cubist circles, when he writes that "for the painter there is no other light than in color… One need only see, at the Orangerie, to what point the love of this phenomenon led Claude Monet—to pictorial suicide. The Ophelia of painting, his soul roams without glory in a shroud of water lilies."[5] To allude to Ophelia in the context of the *Nymphéas* has a significance which goes beyond the mere pleasure of making a facile literary analogy. Lhote himself may have borrowed the idea from an article by Raymond Escholier (in *Le Figaro,* Nov. 19, 1922), who was among the first to announce the project of the installation at the Orangerie. The allusion to this Shakespearian character takes on its full meaning here; the "Pale Ophelia, white like a great lily" (Rimbaud) is indeed a human figure which disappears into the watery depths and vegetation, as in the painting by Millais. Escholier speaks of the "colored poems, dedicated by Monet to the glory of still waters and to the strange flowers that bloom there… *Absent one, I find you…* Hippolytus's words to the fair Aricia, how can one not address them to the shade of Ophelia in contemplating the Water Lilies of Giverny." He accentuates this idea of a presence-absence, of the dissolution of a living being in fluid appearances, by quoting Geffroy, who may well have been the first to speak of Ophellia in connection with Monet's Water Lilies: "The pale figure of Ophelia is about to glide on the water… and then everything—images and thoughts—returns to the void."

Georges Grappe, who knew Monet's work well and who had been received by him at Giverny in 1919 at his own request, also evokes "the shimmering and rising rosaces of the *Nymphéas,* floating, like Ophelia, on the pond at Giverny." (G. Grappe, Monet, Paris, 1941, p. 48). But finally, might it not have been Monet himself who first mentioned the name of Ophelia to his visitors?

Claude Monet himself, as well as his most authorized spokesmen, Geffroy and Clemenceau, seems to have wanted to deny in advance any pretension in the *Nymphéas* to abstraction. The underlying idea throughout Clemenceau's book is that Monet's entire work, and especially the *Nymphéas,* was only the translation of what Monet saw: "Monet can paint nothing more than what he sees." (1928, p. 80). This insistence becomes suspect in the end. Did Monet, and those close to him, sense that other painters, in taking his discoveries to their ultimate consequences, would one day completely invert its spirit?

If it seemed as if he were breaking away, however slightly, from "reality", would this not be giving an argument in support of his detractors of the heroic early period? Monet had not forgotten the fierce criticism of the years between 1870-1880 (he had even assembled and held onto a collection of news clippings, which he later gave to Gustave Geffroy). During the early years of Impressionism, Monet and his friends had been dragged through the mud, on the pretext that their paintings showed nothing at all and that they looked like "smeared palettes." Monet was

5. "Monet et Picasso", *N.R.F.,* 1932, reedited as *Les invariants plastiques,* Paris, 1967, pp. 82-83.

2nd Room, South Wall
Clear Morning with Willows
Three adjoining panels of W. 425 each, i.e. total W. 1,275
Inv. 20106

Thanks to water, at the same time transparency,
iridescence, and mirror, Monet became the indirect painter
of what we cannot see.

PAUL CLAUDEL
Journal, 1904-1932,
Paris, t. I, p. 778, 1968

Amazing painting, without lines or edges, a canticle without words, a work in which the painter has no subject other than himself.

LOUIS GILLET

Monet painted the action of the universe in its workings (…),
this drama crowned by the blinding, fiery flash of the setting sun
in the withered reeds of wintertime marshlands, from which
the enchanting flowers of spring will be reborn, in preparation
in the unfathomable depths of eternal renewals.

GEORGES CLEMENCEAU
Claude Monet, *Les Nymphéas,*
Paris, 1928, p. 54

Opposite:
Morning with Willows (detail)

2nd Room, South Wall
Clear Morning with Willows
Three adjoining panels of W. 425 each, i.e. total W. 1,275
Inv. 20106

"We see to what point the painting of the late Monet was a thing of the mind [chose mentale]. *This already thought-out composition, Monet in no way considered setting himself up by the pond to reproduce it; he had a contractor come and build him a new studio: 'blind walls with no other opening than the door; a skylight along two-thirds of the roof.'(…)*

Great lashes for the riverbank reeds or rushes, wooly verticals for the willows of the second room, small vertical lashes for the willow leaves, the rough-hewn surfaces of the upside-down clouds, the more or less long, more or less animated horizontals of the surface of the water, great enveloping paraphs for the leaves of the water lilies, with bright patches for the flowers; we are in the presence of a whole system of signs.

The raising of the horizon, already very noticeable before, is now absolute, the sky or the far-off distance now appear only as an inversion, and the surface of the water rises toward the vertical all around us, which creates the illusion of flying or of diving (…)

Of the usual landscape, Monet has kept only a few signs.
The surface of the water takes these elements, animates them,
brings out scores of properties in them. But all of this can occur
only because there is already something which defines the
canvas as the surface of a germinative and flowering water,
because of the water lilies through which all of the signs become
legible.

In the real pond at Giverny, the water would have turned the world
upside-down even if there had been no flowers, but in the final
work representation appears only by their presence. They are the
nymphs of sources who have come all the way to the heart of the city
to make us turn topsy-turvy."

MICHEL BUTOR
Art de France, 1963, pp. 298-300
© Editions Hermann

Water Lilies, Evening Effect, 1907,
Paris, Musée Marmottan

surely traumatized by such critiques, and on the eve of the First World War, Impressionism, to say nothing of its offshoots, had still not completely found favor with public opinion.

Monet's attitude, supported by Clemenceau and Geffroy, who shared his ideology, is related to the Realist aesthetic, or rather to Realism as an aesthetic. Realism, and its underlying rationalism, was the prevailing ideology of the second half of the 19th century. Those who were independent enough to liberate themselves from it were few and far between; and it was only at the end of the century that it effectively began to be questioned and that a place could be given to imagination, dreams, and the inner world. Thus around the turn of the century, the Realist myth was still going strong; artists insisted on working after reality, on representing reality—with the illusion of not transposing it. As far as aesthetics were concerned, this was one of the most firmly-rooted convictions in the collective mentality; and it was the very negation of the work of the artist.

It is easier, therefore, to understand Monet's activity of the last thirty years of his life, during which he devoted the greater part of his time and energy—not to

Opposite:
Clear Morning with Willows (detail)

93

André Masson,
Marshes,
Paris, Centre Georges Pompidou,
Musée national d'art moderne

mention his recently-acquired financial means—not so much to painting, as to arranging and constantly transforming his garden and water-lily pond. In order to paint what he wanted to paint, without slipping into the unrealism of abstraction, he created his own models, the garden and the pond, which he reproduced and interpreted in his paintings. There was an artistic creation on two levels here. Just as Cézanne arranged fruits and pitchers on a table before painting, Monet, on a wholly other scale, with an entirely different constancy and wealth of significance, for more than thirty years arranged his garden before rendering it in paint. In setting up his garden as his fancy dictated, and then reproducing it seemingly objectively, Monet was practicing abstract painting on a secondary level.

Apart from the artists who understood, consciously or not, Monet's role as a precursor, there were a few critics who took note of it as well. When Octave Mirbeau wrote in 1912: "Henceforth, no painter will be able to free himself from the problems resolved or posed by Monet" (Preface to *Monet, Venise,* exhibit, cat., Paris, Bernheim-Jeune, 1912), it is not sure that he was thinking of the newly-developing abstract painting. But Mirbeau was familiar enough with the art movements in Paris to be able to situate Monet exactly.

More remarkable is the lucidity of Louis Gillet (1876-1943). An intelligent and open art historian and critic who concerned himself mostly with the art of the past,

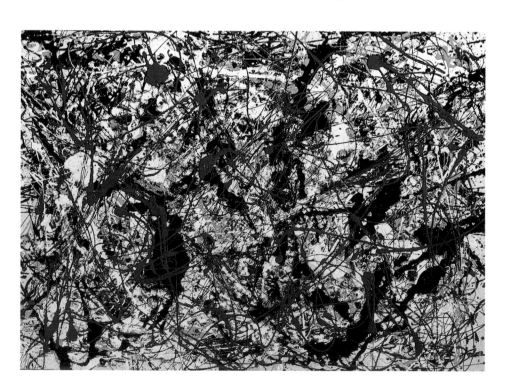

Jackson Pollock,
Painting, 1948,
Paris, Centre Georges Pompidou,
Musée national d'art moderne

94

Georges Mathieu,
*Public Magnificence on the Occasion of
the Birth of Thierry d'Alsace*, 1960
Private collection

Gillet wrote his first text on the Water Lilies in 1909, that is, *before* the very first works of abstract art[6]. Louis Gillet, before Mirbeau and in more general terms, situated the Water Lilies not in the diachronic development of Monet's work, but in a synchronic "section" of the painting of the turn of the century and of the conceptual problems faced by the Cubists and the first abstract painters: "I will leave aside the challenge of showing a view of what is above from below, the problem raised by the intersection of three or four planes, or rather the obligation under which the artist was to represent all of them on an unreal plane: a painter could not have accumulated more paradoxes… Pure abstraction can go no further. Nothing but the free play of the imaginative faculties, the simple combination of forms for the pleasure of it—in the category of art. All of the most exquisite things, the arabesque, the decoration of a vase, a carpet from Herat or Khorassan—the things that are the most conventionalized and simplified, those which are the least incarnate, and which partake the most of music, number, and geometry, do not surpass the charming idealism of the Water Lilies. The artist's thought has reached its highest degree of spiritualization." (Louis Gillet, *La Revue hébdomadaire,* August 21, 1909). If we recall that in 1909 abstract art had yet to be born (even if, in retrospect, its appearance seems logical), then we can only express astonishment at Gillet's perspicacity. He edited his text for publication in a book in 1927 which featured two more essays on Monet in which the non-representational interpretation of the Water Lilies is explicit.

Clemenceau may not have known much about the work of Kandinsky or of Mondrian, but he was astute enough to have had the intuition of one of the most crucial changes in the history of art. He commented on Gillet's text from a diametrically opposed point of view and rejected its conclusion: "No painter has ever negated matter more resolutely", and very clearly stated: "My disagreement with M. Louis Gillet concerns philosophy, not art," then went on to say: "I sincerely admire his perception of the Water Lilies and the pleasant literary transposition which he gives us of them, but how could I concur with the tormented simplicity of this statement: "To admire the enchantment produced by light and the texture of time, to gaze upon the veil of lies, to stretch across a form the miracle of appearances, these are things of which Monet does not tire." There is no possible meeting ground between this metaphysic of the unknown and Monet's spontaneous impulse, which is, not to support a thesis against which the man and his brush could only have rebelled, but to sacrifice all to the expression of *that which is*, to the degree to which he can attain this."

At the time of the opening of the Orangerie to the public (1927), the abstract, or non-representational, interpretation of the *Nymphéas* was expressed only allu-

6. It was probably Louis Gillet who first drew the attention of his friend Charles Péguy (who published his text on the French Primitives in *Cahiers de la Quinzaine,* 7e cahier, VIe serie, 1904) to Monet. As a general rule, Péguy showed little interest in painting; yet he devoted an important passage in *Clio* (1912) to the *Nymphéas* (see p. 110 and 117).

95

sively, and by those of a strongly intuitive bent. It is true that abstract art had been around for only fifteen years, and that it was still largely foreign to Parisian art circles. Raymond Régamey, a young art historian who later became a Dominican monk, placed the *Nymphéas* in the context of a coherent effort by Monet: "It seems as if he were as interested in a leaf as in a dress, in a dress as much as in a face. Thus a sort indifference to the relative value of objects begins to manifest itself, an indifference which, at the beginning, appears to be the submission of a realist to every stimulus falling on his retina, and which, by an imperceptible and logical evolution, will become the whimsical power of the visionary who lends to things the appearance that he wishes." And, "His language differs more and more from nature, replaces it, and yet at the same time pretends to be more and more like it."

As for Paul Claudel, who visited the *Nymphéas* shortly after the opening of the Orangerie in 1927, he remarked: "Monet, at the end of his long life, after having studied all of the answers that the various motifs of nature could bring to the question of light in terms of colored assemblages, finally turned to that most docile, that most yielding of the elements, water—all at once transparency, iridescence, and mirror. Thanks to water, he became *the indirect painter of what we cannot see.*" (*Journal,* July 8, 1927, Paris, vol. I, 1968, p. 778.)

Claudel and Régamey belong to the same spiritual (spiritualized) family as Louis Gillet. This was certainly not the case with Meyer-Schapiro, who proceeded according to the methods of art history. In a text called *The Nature of Abstract Art* (1937), he remarked that the *Nymphéas* were "close to a certain manner of abstract art" (*Marxist Quarterly,* No. 1, January-March, 1937, p. 78.)

It was not before the fifties that this idea was brought up again by a painter, André Masson, a good judge, who wrote several texts on Monet and on the *Nymphéas,* and by critics specialized in abstract art: Léon Degrand, Pierre Restany, Jean-Dominique Rey. The comparisons by then no longer involved only the beginnings of abstract art, but also what constituted, after 1950, a new wave of abstraction, both in Europe and in the United States[7]; variously referred to as Abstract or Lyrical Expressionism, or Action Painting. Comparisons with Pollock, Tobey, or Sam Francis, or with Bazaine, Mathieu, or Masson himself, have by now become commonplace, as have those with Bonnard, who, as we know, was a great admirer of Monet.

Rapid brushwork which, rather than defining contours, expresses the very act of painting, the complete freedom of creation, the abandonment of traditional easel painting and its constraints, the use of oversize formats, these were all characteristics which many American artists may have borrowed from the *Nymphéas,* and not just the action painters (Sam Francis, Ad Reinhardt, Morris Louis, Philip Guston, Barnett Newman, Clifford Still). The latter wrote a text in 1944 already stressing the importance of the Impressionists, and in 1953, he debated with the Museum of Modern Art, which had reproached him with having "mishandled" their historic contribution[8]. The installation at the Orangerie, or the spectacular exhibition of large Water Lilies canvases in the United States, were seen as environments in themselves, and brought about the complete defocalization of painting (an idea taken up by Delaunay, and more recently, by the "Support-Surface" group).

"It was only with Monet", André Masson wrote, "that painting took a different turn. He blasted all of the barriers, doing away with the very idea of form that had dominated us for millenia." (Exhibition cat., Chicago Art Institute, 1975, p. 13.)

The issue of the abstract character of the *Nymphéas* converges with that of their decorative character. The very size of the large canvases, Monet's wish to install them on a wall in a given context and in a fixed order, led many observers to comment on the change of scale and even to see an actual transformation in Monet's work. Georges Rivière, a friend and defender of Monet and Renoir from the outset, as well

7. Franz Meyer presented a detailed study of this question in the catalogue of the 1986 exhibition *Claude Monet: Nymphéas, Impression, Vision* at the Kunstmuseum, Basle, published under the general editorship of Christian Geelhaar (French translation, Paris, 1988). Franz Meyer's contribution was entitled *The "Monet Revival"* and dated from the 1950s.

8. B. Newman, "The Problem of the Subject," written around 1944, French trans, in *Barnett Newman,* exhibition catalogue, Grand-Palais, Paris, 1972.

Water Lilies at Giverny, 1917,
Nantes, Musée des Beaux-Arts

as their admirers Mirbeau and Gustave Kahn, pointed out that, in their beginnings, they had indeed tried their hand at "large-scale" works and that only the incomprehension of the official milieux had prevented them from realizing murals. Even before the opening of the Orangerie, more than one critic stressed the importance of having a "decoration" from Monet's brush. Need we recall also the particular active interest that certain painters of the next generation (the Nabis, Delaunay, Gleizes…) took in mural painting?

Curiously enough, this aspect of Monet's work was to encounter reservations on the part of some whom one would have expected to be more open and prepared to ignore the pejorative connotation which the term "decorative" had at the time. We have already touched on Lhote's critique (see p.76). Jacques-Emile Blanche, the defender of all of the avant-gardes, but not without reservations when it came to evaluating the painters of the Impressionist movement, in his discussion of the *Nymphéas* spoke of wallpaper and of the *"trompe-l'œil* of panoramas", and added, "it would be a disservice to the modesty of Monet to compare, as some have done, these swirls of elephantisiacal petals, these avalanches of corollas, this orgy of silken specimens—the delirium of a flower collector who has withdrawn into his oasis for good—with the *Heliodorus* of Delacroix or his *Sainte Geneviève of Paris.* (Propos de peintre, 3ᵉ série, *De Gauguin a la Revue Nègre,* Paris, 1928).

There are other examples of incomprehension which argue indirectly in favor of the non-realism of the *Nymphéas.* For instance, there is a little-known text by Alexander Benois, who was one of the first decorators for the Ballets Russes, in which he evokes, on the occasion of the 1931 Monet retrospective at the Orangerie, his "erstwhile ecstasies", at Durand-Ruel's gallery, over paintings from the early years or from the Argenteuil period; his lack of comprehension regarding the *Nymphéas* is complete: "What a strange and truly pathetic climax to the career of the creator of the *Woman in Green* and the *Luncheon on the Grass*!.. What vanity reduced him to dealing with such problems of monumental decoration when he had absolutely no talent for it." (*Alexandre Benois réfléchit,* Moscow, 1968, pp.334-355).

The word "decorative" is again used as a reproach by the great aesthetician Eugenio d'Ors: "A seascape which could be inverted, for example, would be a bad painting. Turner himself—daring though he may have been in his luminous phantasmagorias—never ventured to paint a reversible marine landscape, that is, one in which the sky could be taken for the water and the water for the sky. And if the Impressionist Monet did just that, in his equivocal series of Water Lilies, we could say that he found his punishment in his crime; for in the history of art, Monet's Water Lilies never have, and never will, be considered as a normal product; rather a caprice, which, although it may appeal to our sensitivity for a moment, does not deserve to be ennobled by being admitted into the archives of our memory. An ephemeral divertissement; a self-repeating object which already has its place among the purely decorative in the productions of the industrial arts; a cousin of the arabesques, of the tapestries, of the plates of Faenza; a thing, finally, which one sees without looking, apprehends without thought, and forgets without regret". (*La Vie de Goya,* Paris, 1928, p. 179).

Even at the time of the opening of the Orangerie, therefore, men whom one would have expected to be more penetrating did not grasp the break represented by the *Nymphéas.* Mentalities have since evolved—yet not without reticence. In 1931, Giuseppe Marchiori set the *Nymphéas* in a historial perspective: "… the *Nymphéas* today proclaim the vital force which drove Impressionism and which enabled it to attain such peaks, beyond the laws which governed painting, at time when Cubism had already become history, and as movements were succeeding one another by the score, at the whim of our century so given to experiments," (*Corriere Padano,* July 21, 1931), whereas a few years later, L. Venturi, although a historian of Cézanne and of Impressionism, was more restrictive and concluded that the *Nymphéas* were "Monet's most serious artistic mistake" (quoted by J. Rossi Bertolatti, *Monet,* Paris, 1981).

The Poetics of the Nymphéas

In imagining the *Nymphéas,* first of all, and then in realizing them, Monet demonstrated his independence vis à vis of a tradition from which it seemed he had descended.

Sensitivity to nature had regained importance with Rousseau, Chateaubriand, and Romanticism. In painting, the English, Corot, Millet, and the Barbizon group, as early as the mid-19th century, had given particular attention to the landscape, more often than not a landscape characterized by rustic or wild elements. The Impressionists went even further, using the theme of the landscape as the primary support for their revolutionary efforts. Thus, by the end of the 19th century, it was no longer a rediscovery, but a given. The only truly novel feature was the need for a respite from the city, which was easy enough to satisfy for a long time. In *Les Misérables,* for example, city-dwellers could still go out to the country for the day or even for a few hours.

For the artists of the turn of the century, even more than for the Impressionists, nature was a primary source for experiments in style. One need only compare the same beach in Normandy as treated by Monet, Seurat, and Marquet, to see that style prevails above the exact rendition of the subject. As for Art Nouveau, a large part of its inspiration came from plant and floral forms.

The need to get away was particularly widespread at the end of the century. Gauguin's life (and work) is one of the most obvious demonstrations of this search for escape through exoticism, which was expressed also in the literary works of Jules Verne, Pierre Loti, and R.L. Stevenson, then being published in illustrated editions. But there are other forms of escape for which nature is the vehicle too. The *Nymphéas* evoke a sort of timeless nature, a primitive chaos from which man is absent, and in which the pictoral elements happen to be precisely the four elements of traditional iconography: air, water, earth, and fire.

The impact of Monet's work at the turn of the century was not limited to the watered-down Impressionism which was pouring into the Salons. The passion for light, a sort of sun-drenched hedonism, which filled some of his paintings, is perceptible in a painter such as Cross (who must be considered as one of the sources of Fauvism) and the Fauves themselves, who, generally speaking, dealt with the same themes as the Impressionists. And so there is nothing fortuitous in the fact that a certain number of artists, and particularly the members or future members of the Fauvist group, chose precisely the façade of a Gothic church as a subject not long after Monet had exhibited his *Rouen Cathedrals.* This was the case for Matisse, Signac, Marquet, and a little later, for Robert Delaunay in his views of the Cathedral of Laon.

The very titles which Marquet chose for the works that he presented at the Salon des Indépendants and the Salon d'Automne of 1904 and 1905, distinguishing his views of Notre-Dame Cathedral only by differences in the time of day or weather conditions ("Morning," "Mist," "Full Sunlight…"), constitute nothing less than a duplication of the titles that Monet had chosen for his *Rouen Cathedrals*. Although Marquet does not seem to have acknowledged his source, it is too obvious to be ignored.

On the other hand, when Derain went to London at the request of Ambroise Vollard, the object of his trip, to paint views of the Thames in response to those successfully exhibited by Monet in 1904, was overtly and explicitly stated. Borrowing Monet's freedom of interpretation, his rejection of the anecdotal, and his non-realistic colors, Derain produced a series of pictures of a much more violent and varied temper than Claude Monet's.

The representation of nature in its primary forms (water, light, and vegetation) appears in much of Monet's work, but even more so in the *Nymphéas*. It is perhaps no coincidence that at the time when Monet began to devote himself almost exclusively to this theme many other artists adopted a similar line, at least in certain of their works. There was of course Gauguin, who filled his canvases with tropical vegetation; but this was also the case for Cézanne, in a number of his views of *Château Noir* and, more generally, of the environs of Aix. We would point out that this fusion between air, water, the mineral, and the organic into a sort of biosphere, appears already in one of the rare late works by Cézanne that can be dated with certainty, the *View of the Lake of Annecy* of 1896 (Courtauld Collection, London), which is just anterior to the very first Water Lilies. Other paintings, such as *The Pine Branch* (Paris, Petit Palais) or *The Park at Château Noir* in the Orangerie, to mention only two examples, partake of same spirit.

The tropical landscapes of Henri Rousseau, in which the vegetation constitutes a sort of all-over pattern which almost completely covers the sky, were also painted around 1900-1910 for the most part. The list of these conjunctions could be lengthened to include, for instance, Redon's frescoes at Fontfroide, certain landscapes by Gustav Klimt or Augusto Giacometti, Léger's *Nudes in the Forest,* or Picasso's *Dryads* of 1908. Is it necessary to speak of influence on this account? The concept of influence, used to construct genealogical trees of sorts, has been much abused in the history of art. It is more prudent, and perhaps more meaningful, to note these convergences and to consider that they may extend to the literature and poetry of the period; they are also practically contemporaneous with the elaboration of Teilhard de Chardin's evolutionist theories and of Paul Claudel's *Légende de Prakriti.*

In fact, this taste for natural motifs, and especially plant motifs, had been a constant feature of Monet's work. It is true that until 1870 his production included, apart from landscapes, many portraits, still lifes, and interior scenes. But afterwards, his more ambitious works, if only by their size (the *Women in the Garden* and the *Luncheon on the Grass),* show him to be concerned with associating man and nature; he did not shrink from tackling this pictorial subject which many a painter, Manet for one, had a difficult time mastering; he succeeded in harmoniously associating figures in city dress, trees, and (for example, in *The Terrace at Sainte-Adresse*), flowers and the sea. This theme of city-dwellers indulging in their pastimes, so often treated by most of the Impressionists and by Seurat, furnished him the pretext for a great number of works in which man's place was progressively reduced. Starting with the 1880s, with the exception of his *Women* with *Parasols* and his series of *Boats on the Epte,* the human figure became virtually absent from his work or was reduced to a vague silhouette; the principal subjects of his compositions then were the sun, clouds, water, and plant life. Whenever he could, it was to them that he entrusted the animation of his canvases: clouds floating by, poplars bending in the wind, water that is rarely still, but agitated by waves, as at Belle-Ile, or transformed into the chaotic ice floes of the debacles.

Water Lilies, circa 920,
New York,
The Museum of Modern Art,
Mrs. Simon Guggenheim Fund

He endowed natural elements normally considered inert with the living traits that he seems to have refused to human beings. Thus, in accordance to a certain logic, or, in a manner of speaking, to a certain intensification of Monet's choice of subject-matter, he concentrated his work on the sole theme of the water-lily pond, where water, air, and vegetation merge to such an extent that, very often, it is impossible to distinguish what, in this colored mist, represents willow leaves, water plants, or simply reflections on the water. The fourth element of traditional cosmogony, fire, is also there; not directly, but in the flame-like forms which Monet very often gave to the branches of the willow tree, or in the implicit presence of the sun.

It might seem arbitrary to relate this quasi-pantheistic vision to that of Claudel or of Teilhard de Chardin, nor does it seem to concord with the religious skepticism—not to say atheism—which Monet seems always to have professed. And yet, although he may have foregone his Catholic instruction and not been involved much in any positivist religion, there is no reason to doubt this pantheistic spirit, which was shared by his friend Georges Clemenceau.

It might come as a surprise to find Clemenceau associated with what is virtually a religious interpretation of the *Nymphéas.* As a politician, Clemenceau, who was notoriously anti-clerical, is known to have been particularly active in the anti-religious struggles of the 3rd Republic. In the texts in which he publicly stated his religions opinions, he consistently manifested his hostility to Christianity, and more generally to the positivist religions. On the other hand, he no-less overtly subscribed to a sort of Deism which stressed the forces of Nature and Life, and found a satisfactory expression of his religious affinities in certain Hindu beliefs and in certain myths from Antiquity, in particular that of the god Pan; in fact, he gave one of his books the title of *Le Grand Pan* (1896): it is a series of articles on the most diverse subjects in which one would have expected to find an introduction in a political vein, but instead there is a long confession of his humanist and semi-religious beliefs. These ideas, which could already be detected between the lines of his M.D. thesis in 1865, were taken up again in *Au soir de la pensée* (1927), a book which constitutes his spiritual testament. Most of the biographies of Clemenceau scarcely mention this aspect of his thought, yet it apparently meant a great deal to him.

Could it be that Clemenceau influenced Monet in this realm of ideas? It would be simpler to suppose that the two men shared common views[1]. In any event, it seems to us that Clemenceau was a better interpreter of Monet's real intentions than Gustave Geffroy. The latter is customarily considered as having been the

1. A thesis on the artistic role and tastes of Georges Clemenceau is in preparation at the Ecole du Louvre [but does not seem to have been published (2006)].

101

artist's special confidant. It would seem, however, that Monet used Geffroy, and Ambroise Vollard too, for that matter, to compose a certain image of himself as a gruff, instinctive painter, painting without resorting to reflection or calculation— a closer study, however, reveals that not only the *Nymphéas* but the entire body of Monet's work attest to intentions and a spirit of experimentation which bears little relation to the Monet portrayed by Geffroy.

The abandonment of reality, or rather the simple transcription of appearances, in favor of a deeper reality, such as it appears in the wealth of light, water, and vegetation in the *Nymphéas,* was not a new attitude on Monet's part. For too long, Impressionism has been interpreted simply as a sort of outdoors picnic, expressing the *joie de vivre* of Parisians in the country. It was also—and especially in Monet— a quest for that most subtle, impalpable, and changing aspect of the visible world: light. It was a far cry from the prosaic or anecdotal transcription of everyday life or nature to which painters of the preceding generation, such as Courbet and the members of the Barbizon group, had limited themselves, or rather appeared to limit themselves: yet Geffroy suggests—somewhat hastily—that Monet subscribed to the same aesthetic principles.

If Monet belonged to the scientific and intellectual currents of his time, and even if, with his painter's intuition, he sometimes anticipated them, it was not by trying to apply the theories of Chevreul, Helmholtz, or Rood. There is no evidence that he delved overmuch in their books; they had more of an impact on Seurat, Signac, and the Neo-Impressionists. There is no trace in Monet of a halfbaked scientism; nowhere the idea that the work of the artist may be rationalized or systematized.

Curiously enough, this gap between the prevailing theories and actual convictions was sensed by the young Léon Blum, who was then trying his hand as a critic. Referring to the positions of Marcelin Berthelot, whose son had been one of his childhood friends, he wrote: "The various aesthetic doctrines which came into being around 1865, under the impulsion of the scientific movement and of the scientific group of which Mr. Berthelot was one of the most prominent figures, were all based *on* the selfsame error that Mr. Berthelot so clearly dispelled, and that is, that the results or the methods of science are entirely transposable or useable in the realm of art. The Impressionist school in painting, which assembled some admirable artists, developed from Chevreul's theories on the division of colors and the separation of the solar spectrum into simple colors (…) This is not the time to examine to what extent these errors hindered the genius of a Monet or a Zola. But it is a remarkable thing that they were not shared by a scientist, one of their friends or contemporaries, in whom an enthusiastic faith in Science would have made them more natural." (Reedited in *En lisant,* 1906, p. 335.)

On the other hand, Clemenceau did not hesitate to see in the *Nymphéas* a "representative interpretation" of matter, such as modern physics conceived it. It is worth quoting the entire passage: "… the painter reveals to us, as if by an ultramicroscopic lighting, elemental depths which, without him, we would never have known! Are we not here very close to a representative interpretation of *Brownian movement*? Needless to say, there is a great distance between art and science. But there is at the same time the great unity of cosmic phenomena, of which the painter gives us, instead of a direct vision, an interpretation endowed with an overwhelming feeling for beauty, in which pure knowledge comes only after painstaking observation."

Réne Huyghe has analyzed in detail this profound accord between Impressionism—of which the *Nymphéas* are the ultimate achievement—and science: "A new feeling for nature appeared then: everything which in it evoked immobi-

The water-lily pond with irises,
Zurich, Kunsthaus

lity, or stability, was eliminated: it was looked to more and more for the fluid and the impalpable; it lost its properties of weight, density, and firmness—all at once its content, form, and tangibility—to be dissolved into an imponderable appearance." Huyghe, who also quotes Clemenceau, further noted "… there was a more intimate relation between the thought of the artist, the scientist, and the philosopher at the century's end. Around them, they renounced nature and its traditional prerogatives: but within, they renounced the hereditary limits of logic (…) the novel with Proust and painting with the Impressionists made analogous efforts to shake off the mechanization which intelligence imposed on the elusive and ineffable truth of life and to reestablish a spontaneous contact with it. (…) Bergson in his philosophy, Proust in his novels, Monet in his 'series', are possessed by the idea that neither things, nor our beings remain the same in themselves, endure with their identity intact: each new second brings modifications which transform their very nature." (R. Huyghe, *La relève du réel, Impressionisme et Symbolisme,* Paris, 1974).

It is obvious that there is no contradiction—on the contrary—between this approach to the late works of Monet and the purely pictoral undertaking which led him to an ever-greater renunciation of legibility. The same *Haystacks* which Mirbeau, who was little inclined to gratuitous lyricism or pomposity, qualified as "such poignant pictures, of a truly cosmic grandeur" (*Journal,* April 20, 1900), at the same time led Kandinsky to discover the possibility of painting without representation.

R. Régamey (see p. 96) noted that: "It seems as if he were as interested, if not more, in a leaf as in a dress, in a dress as much as in a face. Thus a sort of indifference to the relative value of objects begins to manifest itself, an indifference which seems to be, in the beginning, the submission of the realist to every stimulus falling on his retina." (1927). Valéry (speaking of Corot, it is true) had formulated similar remarks. "The artist's observation can attain almost mystical depths. The objects in the light lose their names: areas of shadow and light give rise to systems and problems of their own which derive from no science, which refer to no practice, but which obtain their entire being and their value from a singular accord between the soul, the eye, and the hand of someone who was born to surprise and to produce them within himself." (*Pieces sur l'art,* Paris, 1934).

We could have quoted more of the same, especially from Clemenceau: even this impenitent rationalist regularly resorted to an unexpected vocabulary: *infinite, emotion, cosmic:* Thus, "Monet painted the action of the universe in its workings, creating and perpetuating itself through momentary steps surprised upon the reflecting surfaces of his lily pond. This drama crowned by the blinding, fiery flash—in the last panel of the Tuileries—of the setting sun in the withered rushes of wintertime marshlands, from which the enchanting flowers of spring will be reborn, in preparation in the unfathomable depths of eternal renewals." (1928, p. 54). It reads more like a passage from Claudel or Teilhard de Chardin!

Was Monet's choice of the water lily as the virtually exclusive subject of his work due only to horticultural considerations? What other artist—with the same ambition as Monet (and who is not Redouté)—would have devoted more than twenty years of this life to a single species of plants? The matter is still more peculiar, for although plant life always had an important place in his work, the formal representation of flowers, in bouquets or still lifes, occurs only exceptionally in Monet.

There was more to it, however, than just the representation of the most common of ornamental aquatic plants, the water-lily ("*nénuphar*" in the French text); and to have called them by the more rare designation of *nymphéa* (or the common white water lily, equivalent in poetic evocation to the English word "lotus", a term applied to exotic species of water lilies—Trans.), was already a departure from ordinary terminology. In the poetic language of the 19th century, the water lily, oddly enough, had dark and malefic connotations:

"At night the elves emerge
Their robes wet at the hem
To drag beneath the water lily
Their O so weary waltzer."[2]
Théophile Gautier

Maeterlinck, who was discovered and greatly admired by Mirbeau, Monet's friend, speaks in his *Serres chaudes* (lit. "hot-houses") (1896) of the "dreary water-lilies of pleasure." But it was Victor Hugo in particular who, in the very first lines of *Le Sacre* (The Consecration), on the melody of Malbrouck, or the aria of Cherubini, used it with its fullest significance:

"In the horrid cemetery
Paris trembles, O sorrow, O misery!
In the horrid cemetery
Quivers the water lily."[3]
(*Les Châtiments*, 1853)

In the remarkably modern commentary on the language of this poem which Charles Péguy gives in *Clio* (1912), he underlined this negative connotation of the water lily, and although he rarely dealt with painting, added a few lines, without mentioning Monet, on "that very great modern and contemporary painter who painted twenty-seven or thirty-five times his famous *Nymphéas*." We have already mentioned (p. 21 and 95) that it was probably Louis Gillet who informed Péguy about Monet, his methods and his work. For Péguy, like for Hugo in his barbs against "*Napoléon-le-Petit*", the value attached to the word water lily is obvious: "This punishment of punishments, this punishment of the tomb and of the resurrection of the crime is entirely conducted through the power of that funereal rhyme and with the threat of that secretly awful word: the *nénuphar*." (*Clio*). Still in the context of Hugo and Monet, Péguy has Clio ask herself: "I would give much (…) to know right now what difference there is, or should be, between *Nénuphars* and *Nymphéas*, if there is one." (see p. 110 and 117).

2. "C'est la nuit que les elfes sortent
Avec leur robe humide au bord
Et sous les nénuphars emportent
Leur valseur de fatigue mort."

3. "Dans l'affreux cimetière
Paris tremble, ô douleur, ô misère!
Dans l'affreux cimetière
Frémit le nénuphar."

Monet was probably aware of the dark associations of the term *"nénuphar"* when he chose to refer to his plants by the scientific term of *"nymphéas"*, less common, but almost synonymous, and definitely more evocative. In botanical terminology, *Nymphaea* designates the genus of the *Nymphaeacae* family which includes water lilies and lotuses. There are species of water lilies that grow wild (in the ponds of Rambouillet, for example) and cultivated varieties, like those of Giverny.

Put into general circulation thanks to Monet, the term of *nymphéa* was free of malefic connotations, and evoked words like *nymphaeum* (a sacred cave with a spring) or nymph; according to mythology, the water lily was born of a nymph who drowned herself out of love for Hercules, and could well have been represented in Poussin's *Empire de Flore*. Michel Butor wrote that "[Monet] is imploring the divinities of the springs." We have also seen how, by 1930, allusions to Ophelia had become commonplace (p. 76).

Marcel Proust, writing at the same time as Péguy (and alluding also to Monet without naming him), in *Swann's Way* (1913), intuitively, and probably unconsciously, made a distinction between the two terms. The narrator describes the Vivonne flowing near the Château de Guermantes, and observes water lilies (*nénuphars* in the original) which he compares to neurasthenics, "trapped in the mechanism of their ills and manias," and also to "those wretches whose singular torment, repeated indefinitely throughout eternity, excited the curiosity of Dante." The nuance is not the same as in Hugo, but it is not much more pleasant. And then the tone changes completely, as the narrator speaks of *"Nymphéas"* which a landowner "who had indulged in the cultivation of aquatic plants, which he grew in the little ponds created by the Vivonne." Under his pen, these *"nymphéas"* called forth only terms of admiration and poetry; they partake of "the kaleidoscope of an attentive, silent, and mobile contentment" (see the passage in its entirety p. 26 and 31). Between the cultivated varieties and those in the wild, there must not have been much difference in their aspect, color, or motion. The change in terms entails, or follows from, a complete change of meaning.

Although Monet was very often mentioned in his novels and in his correspondence, it seems that Proust never actually visited Giverny, but there is an allusion to it in the preface to Ruskin's book, *Sésame et les lys* (1906, p. 33). In an article published in *Le Figaro* on June 15, 1907, after a long discussion on Gustave Moreau, Proust formulated, like a hypothesis necessary to his exposition: "If… I were one day to see to garden of Claude Monet", and with great insight remarks that this garden, of which he must have had some idea, is "a real transposition of art, instead of the model for a painting, a painting already executed with nature itself." (Article on *"Les Eblouissements,* par la comtesse de Noailles", reprinted in Essais et articles, Paris, p. 540). In September-October 1907, during a stay at Glisolles, in the Eure, he contemplated a visit to Giverny, but finally decided against it (*Correspondence avec Mme Straus,* Paris, 1936). A letter from October 1908 tells us that he visited the exhibition of *Nymphéas* at Durand-Ruel's gallery in the company of the same Madame Straus. From other allusions gleaned in his correspondence, it would seem that Monet and Proust actually did meet.

Between Proust and Monet, the "affinities"[4] were too numerous and too deep not to have been noticed, if not by Monet[5], then at least by Proust: the same geographical locations (Paris, Ile-de-France, the Normandy coast, Venice), the same affirmation of the creator's independence vis à vis of "models" and of the outside world (thus it was during the bitterest battles of the First World War that Monet painted his most heavenly Water Lilies, and that Proust devoted two hundred pages to a dinner at the Duchess de Guermantes's—yet in their respective correspondence they expressed great anxiety at the war: they grasped the mainstream of

4. A term whose use by King Theodosius gave so much pleasure to M. de Norpois, two characters in Proust's *A la recherche du temps perdu.*

5. A reader of the *Revue blanche,* in which Proust often wrote.

current events in depth, but always via their own imperatives); the same development of the work in an organic way, like a living being sufficient unto itself, breaking through the accepted material and formal norms: easel painting for the *Nymphéas,* and the well-defined novel for the *Recherche,* which unrepentantly disregarded the conventional notions of tomes and volumes (only the old in-12, square-format edition gives an idea of the luxuriant proliferation of the text); and last of all perhaps, the rejection of the work's traditional purpose: representation for painting, and narration for the novel.

This total break with formal conventions and the charisma common to Proust and Monet were noted by Henri de Régnier, whose rare sensitivity destined him to sing the praises of the *Nymphéas* and, at the same time, to become one of the first admirers of Proust's work: give or take a few nuances, his lines written on the occasion of the publication of *Du côté de Guermantes* could be applied to the rooms at the Orangerie: "[It is] one of the most singular and most captivating works of contemporary literature. I use the expression captivating intentionally, for M. Marcel Proust indeed captivates us completely. His power over our attention is so uncanny that the must possess some magical secret. To realize just how much, it should be kept in mind that M. Proust's books are extremely compact, almost without any chapter divisions, the pages filled with dense text, massive paragraphs, volumes whose subject could be summarized in a few mere, *almost insignificant* lines (…) Open a book by M. Marcel Proust and… you will be enthralled by its charm and power. You will find yourself caught in a sort of magic net which is both invisible and strong." (*Le Figaro,* Nov. 28, 1920).

It would be impossible to list here of all the literary and poetic commentaries and allusions generated by the *Nymphéas*—from the poems of H. de Régnier

(*Vestigia flammae*, 1923), whose entire work is filled with water-soaked gardens and scented flowers, to Aragon's intentionally prosaic description in *Aurélien*. We have seen how Péguy, Proust, and Claudel hit upon the essential, sensing the *Nymphéas's* revolutionary status as an artistic creation, perceiving the deep poetic resonances of the closed, yet unbounded world which they formed in themselves. Gaston Bachelard wrote: "If he dared to, a philosopher daydreaming before a water picture by Monet could develop a dialectics of the iris and of the lotus, a dialectics of the straight leaf and of the leaf that is calmly, quietly, heavily resting on the water... The lotus has understood the lesson of calmness given by still water." (*Verve*, VII, 1952, p. 60). In this, he is close to Proust who saw in the water lilies of the Vivonne "the kaleidoscope of an attentive, silent, and mobile contentment", or an "incitation to a reverie on the setting sun."

Was Proust familiar with the article by Roger Marx published in the *Gazette des Beaux-Arts* in June 1909 (pp. 523-532)? Transcribing the thought, if not the very words, of Monet, Marx has him say that for the visitor of the room that he is planning: "His nerves overstrained by work will be able to relax there, as in the restful example of stagnant water; and for one living in it, this room will offer the haven of a peaceful meditation in the middle of a flowered aquarium." Which of course brings to mind Matisse's words: "What I dream of is an art of balance, of purity, of tranquility, without a disturbing or preoccupying subject, which would be, for those who work with their minds—businessmen as well as men of letters, among others—a lenitive, a cerebral tranquilizer, something analogous to a good armchair to relax one's weary limbs." (*"Notes d'un peintre,"* *La Grande Revue,* Sept. 1908). This parallel is all the more striking because *"Notes d'un peintre"* came out just a few months *before* Roger Marx's visit to Monet, and Roger Marx must surely have been acquainted with the text by Matisse.

And lastly, the *Nymphéas* were defined by their own creator, at an early date and once and for all, not as the formal culmination of Impressionism, or even of his whole work (they are that *too),* but as a creation of another kind: they are not paintings for museums, but a door to contemplation and to the sacred. The rooms at the Orangerie are closer to a Romanesque cloister than to a gallery of Impressionist paintings. To mention the testimony of only one person, Ozenfant, whose rigorist and doctrinaire spirit and Constructivist convictions dit not predispose him to any sympathies with Monet. After a visit to the Orangerie, Ozenfant noted in his journal: "Monet devoted his last years to the poetic series of the *Nymphéas* (...) I found myself taking off my hat. When an experience provokes such a decisive reflex, there is no doubt about it; the work is a strong and elevated one. In spite of this apparent superficiality, Monet, like Matisse, attained results as elevated as certain severe works. The chapel-like presentation, the submarine light, contribute to this strong impression; but, all the same, Monet had something to do with it." (*Mémoires 1886-1962,* Paris, 1968, p. 216, entry of June 27, 1931).

Opposite:
Claude Monet in front of the water-lily pond; the japanese bridge is in the background

Opposite:
The Two Willows (detail)

2nd Room, East Wall
The Two Willows
Four adjoining panels of W. 425 each, i.e. total W. 1,700
Inv. 20104

"You were told yesterday at the cahiers about that very great modern and contemporary painter who painted twenty-seven or thirty-five times his famous Nénuphars *or* Nymphéas; *(I would give much, the story says, to know what difference there is, or should be, between* Nénuphars *and* Nymphéas, *if there is one); and who sold them for at least thirty thousand francs each (time). Thirty thousand francs for one, or thirty-one thousand francs. These accounts are never right. I do not tell you this, my friend, I do not remind you of this, from yesterday to today, to urge you treacherously to do a multiplication. (Which in any case would be audacious, for I cannot guarantee either of these or those numbers, first of all because I do not know them (even I the story don't know the whole of it), and if I were to communicate them to you (when I shall know them), I would seem to be (wanting to) designate someone). And so not only do I not reproach him for having sold them for thirty thousand francs the one (I, the story, know a little of what the temporal is); but I do not reproach him any the more for having done them thirty times. Why take him to task for it, when on the contrary the greatest have done as much – and were perhaps great only because of that – when the greatest geniuses have done as much – and were perhaps great geniuses only because of that. – It would be quite ungrateful of me to take him to task for it, for if I am speaking to you of this, it is on the contrary that this great painter not only painted twenty-seven or thirty-five times his admirable* nénuphars, *but he also painted at the same time, thus giving the most perfect example one could imagine, the most succinct case which could be made, the model so to speak, without which one would have had to do it on purpose, the culminating instance, the most appropriate of all examples of this*

*central problem, a truly typical case, the most fully significant and
the most representative example. We are all redoing our famous
Nénuphars. All of us little ones. But the greatest geniuses in the world
never proceeded otherwise. And it is perhaps because of this that
they were geniuses, and the greatest geniuses in the world. Some
expressly and very visibly, the others more mutely, more secretly; the
same ones more or less expressly or more secretly, more or less visibly,
superficially, or in a more interior way so to speak, more deeply,
in a deeper interior, they often did nothing more, they perhaps never
did more than start again their admirable Nénuphars. Some by
painting them; and others by singing them; writing them; telling their
story. One wonders even if that is not the proper course of genius,
 if such is not the order of genius, its technique and its destination:
to give once and for all, as much as possible forever and ever, a certain
temporal resonance. (…) But I do not think that there has ever been
realized a more succinct case, one so marvellously unique, so rare,
so extreme, so perfectly successful as that of these very Nénuphars.
I do not think that there has ever been painted, or sung, or written,
or told the story of one so typical. It poses indeed in all of its beauty,
in all of its case-ness, the problem with which we are dealing, this
central problem. Given the fact that a very great painter painted
twenty-seven or thirty-five times his famous nénuphars, when did
he paint them the best? And you see where this leads for all the others,
all together. Which of these twenty-seven or thirty-five nénuphars
were painted the best? The logical move would be to say: the last,
because he knew more (the most). And me I say: on the contrary, after
all, the first, because he knew less (the least).*"

CHARLES PÉGUY
Clio, 1911, published in *La Grande Revue*,
October 1917, pp. 610-612
© Editions Gallimard

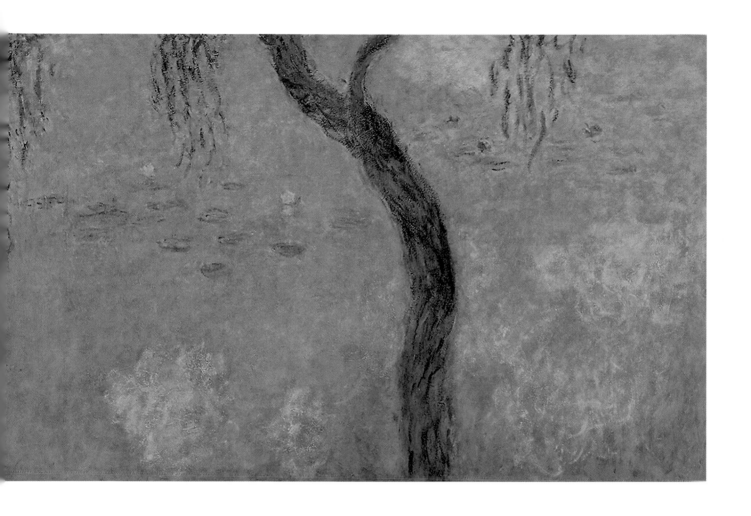

Appendix

The references have been updated (2006).
The abbreviations "LW" refer to Monet's letters published in Wildenstein, 1974, 1991, and "Corr. Clem." to the edition of Clemenceau's letters to Monet, 1993.

Letter from Monet to the *Préfet de l'Eure*

Giverny, July 17, 93

Monsieur le Préfet,

I have the honor of submitting to you a few observations regarding the opposition raised by the municipal council and several inhabitants of Giverny concerning the two inquiries made relative to the request which I have had the honor of addressing to you, in view of obtaining the authorization to create a duct to draw water from the Epte River to feed a pool in which I intend to cultivate aquatic plants.

I would like to point out to you that, under the pretext of public salubrity, the aforementioned opponents have in fact no other goal than to hamper my projects out of pure meanness, as is frequently the case in the country when Parisian landowners are involved: that, for the rest, these opponents, whose number is small in relation to our population, are composed of people whom I do not or no longer employ, such as Mme. Serrurier etc., and that they are acting out of spite and petty vengeance. I dare to hope, *Monsieur le Préfet,* that you will take these reasons into consideration and respond favorably to my request.

I would also like you to know that the aforementioned cultivation of aquatic plants will not have the importance that this term implies and that it will be only a pastime, for the pleasure of the eye, and for motifs to paint; and finally that I am cultivating in this pool only plants such as water lilies, reeds, different varieties of irises which generally grow in a natural state along our river, and that there is absolutely no danger of poisoning the water.

If the villagers remain unconvinced, I am prepared to promise to renew the water of this pool only during the night, when no one is using the water.

I hope that after these explanations you will understand the situation and that you will be able to grant me a favorable response.

You will please pardon the liberty I take in asking you, *Monsieur le Préfet,* to accept the expression of my most distinguished sentiments.

Claude Monet, artist

LW 1219

Letter from Monet to Georges Durand-Ruel

May 28, 1921

Dear Mr. Georges,

I have learned by letter from Mrs. Bernheim that they plan to come with you and your brother, as soon as he returns, that is, in the first half of June, which makes me suppose [sic] that afterwards you will go to Dordogne. I would therefore like to ask you to come for lunch with Mme. G. Durand-Ruel *next Thursday, June 2nd.* It would give us great pleasure. I choose this day because I will be having many visits on the other days.

I would be very obliged to hear from you by return mail.
Please give our cordial best wishes to Mme. Durand-Ruel.
Your very devoted.
Claude Monet

LW 2436

Letter from Clemenceau to Gustave Geffroy

Paris, November 2, 1921

Dear Friend,

On Monet's initiative, negotiations for the donation of the panels have resumed. *We agree on the conditions for both parties.* I want you to know that the credit for this goes to you. But not a word until further orders.

Yours always.
G. Clemenceau

LW 2459

Opposite:
The Two Willows (detail)

Letter from Clemenceau to Monet

Paris, November 2, 1921

My Very Dear Friend,

I have just seen Paul Léon. *Everything* has been arranged according to the conditions that you set down. As you see, I did not go beyond the deadline of three days.

If you wish, we will see you on Tuesday morning. We can leave from my home at 8:30. We can therefore be at your place at ten. We will have to return to Paris for lunch. M. Bonnier, the architect, will be coming along. Also, (strictly between the two of us) I have started negotiations to have your portrait put in the Louvre and Paul Léon is doing his best for this. He was very enthusiastic. *Not a word of this on Tuesday.*

I embrace you and the blue angel.

G. Clemenceau

Corr. Clem., p. 91

Letter from Clemenceau to Monet

Paris, December 14, 1921

Dear Friend,

You are now in the clear, and I have good news for you. I had asked Paul Léon to come to see me this morning. He has just left. *He will do whatever you wish.* We will submit to you the plans which will be signed by both parties, and there will be no room for further discussion. As soon as the budget is passed (in a few days), we will go to work. *There will be no difficulties. No more Bonnier.* Paul Léon has just appointed a new architect from the Louvre who will follow his directions. I am writing this to you with his consent.

So return to your work in peace and leave it to the Gods. Especially, do not catch any more colds. I shall see you as soon as I return. All my incense to the angel of the Lord!

I embrace you with all my heart.

G. Clemenceau

Corr. Clem., p. 94

Letter from Clemenceau to Monet

Paris, December 24, 1921

Dear Friend,

Enclosed is a note from Paul Léon which should satisfy you completely on all points. It is the response to the letter in which I told him about Bonnier's unexpected visit to Giverny.

Now all is well and we shall begin the work. Onward.
Yours always.
G. Clemenceau

Corr. Clem., p. 94

Letter from Clemenceau to Monet

Saint-Vincent-sur-Jard
December 29, 1921

Dear Friend,

As soon as I received your letter, I wrote Paul Léon to tell him what had happened. The simple fact is that he probably had not notified Bonnier yet.

I reminded him that it was with his authorization that I informed you of the new arrangements, and that I wrote you post haste to continue [sic for confirm?] them to you. If need be I will keep you informed of the correspondence. But the commitments are such that they cannot be avoided.

The sea is blooming with foam, and while the blue angel smooths her feathers, me, I feel completely feathered.

I embrace you both all the same.

G. Clemenceau

Corr. Clem., p. 95

Letter from Monet to Marc Elder

Giverny-par-Vernon, Eure
May 8, 1922

My Dear Friend,

A thousand pardons for having left you so long without giving you any news, I have not even thanked you for your delicious wine. It is very bad of me, but the fact is that my door was closed to everyone all winter.

I felt that each day my sight was diminishing and I wanted to take advantage of what little I had left to bring to completion some of my decorations and I was wrong to do so, for I finally had to admit that I was spoiling them and that I was no longer capable of doing anything beautiful, and I destroyed a number of my large panels.

Today, I am almost blind and I have to forego all work. It is hard and quite sad, but that's the way it is: a sad end for all my fine health. In short, all I have left are pastimes. I can have you for lunch whenever you like, if you let me know in advance. You will choose the picture I promised and we will talk.

With best wishes from my stepdaughter to Madame Marc Elder.

I send you both my best wishes.
Your
Claude Monet

LW 2494

Letter from Monet to Marc Elder

Giverny-par-Vernon, Eure
December 2, 1923

Dear Friend,

A few quick lines to let you know that I have received all of your photos, but I never heard you mention photographs that you wanted us to take.

I regret for you that we have not been able […?] more satisfaction.

I would like to know that you are better. But Michel and I are glad to know that you are excited about the automobile.

I have gone back to work and haven't a minute to lose if my panels are to be ready in time.

My cordial best wishes to your wife and to Yvon.

When I am more advanced in my work and the weather is better, we will ask you to come.

Yours.
Claude Monet

LW 2666

Letter from Monet to Marc Elder

Giverny-par-Vernon, Eure
February 25, 1924

Dear Friend,

Do not think that I am forgetting you, not at all, but with my forsaken sight, I am going through hard times. I have to work without stopping if I want to be ready to give my panels to the State. And so I am doing more bad work than good. I destroy what is more or less good.

With this comes a terrible discouragement, for I can tell that I am no longer good for anything, that my life as a painter is over now.

It is not very cheerful and you will understand that I cannot see anyone at the moment.

We often speak of you with my daughter. We all send our best wishes to your wife and to Yvon. I saw that your book was finally announced at Bernheim's.

All yours.
Claude Monet

LW 2671

Letter from Clemenceau to Monet

March 1st, 1924

My Poor Old Crackpot,

I think I like you better when you are stupid. The pleasure of liking you aside, I would wish it to happen less often.

You have come down with a double cataract. This can happen to anyone. You have felt the blow even more sharply because you are a peerless artist, and because you have undertaken with failing sight to do better than with both eyes. What's amazing is that you have succeeded. Such are the elements of your present misfortune.

You have spent your life between crises of success and defiant reactions against yourself. These are the very conditions of your triumph. This continues with the aggravating factor of an overworked retina. You have decided that your work interrupted when you were at the end of your rope would be resumed with half your sight. And you have managed to produce a finished masterpiece (I mean the panel with the cloud) and some marvelous preparations.

After that, Monet said to himself: the only thing to do is to go on. But the Good Lord himself will tell you that you can't make miracles all the time. You are only a man, my friend, and I am very glad of it, for if you were some Good Lord, you would be very boring. Happy imperfection!

You are marking a halt. Whether in art or in science, that is the condition of all activity. In your case, is it attributable to failing eyesight or to the power of creation? I don't know. You may find out which it is in the very near future. I read the very excellent article on you in the *Revue des Deux-Mondes;* it's one of the best things that has been done on you. But since the critics have not seen the panels by you which are such a prodigious assemblage of observation and imagination, the *creation Monétique* aspect has escaped them. In your last panels, I found the same *creative* power taken perhaps even higher. In the preparations sometimes, perhaps another brushstroke, which was without importance. I say no more because I don't know what followed. I see that you are in a state of oscillation, which is not surprising after such an effort. Well, here is my remedy: when the pendulum is at the end of its swing, it swings back. Because of the amazing movement in the brushwork of the *Cloud,* I do not want to take your sight to task. You may be in a better position than anyone to realize this. If you are in doubt, you could take the advice of Coutela, but with what the actual sight is producing, I would not want to rush him.

We can wait a little longer before giving our decision. When P.L. presents himself, which should be soon, for I see that the work is finishing, I will give him arguments to keep him waiting. So get a good hold of yourself, and consent to be only a man made of both force and weakness. I am convinced that you will cross the *great moat of the arena* many more times. Let go of the hands and kick with the spurs. It is easier for me to say this to you, than for you to do it. But you are Monet.

As soon as my cold lets me, I will bring you word of all that is being said.

And then wash your head with my blessing.

G. Clemenceau

Corr. Clem., p.147

Letter from Monet to Marc Elder

Giverny-par-Vernon
October 6, 1924

Dear Friend,

I am guilty of not having giving you much news in so long and of not having thanked you for sending me your latest book.

You will excuse me, won't you, when you learn of the complete discouragement that is killing me.

My poor eyesight is the cause, the only cause, without it I would still be valiantly and ardently at work, while everything that I touch, I spoil, I lose, it's disheartening. Please excuse these complaints and believe in my friendship. My daughter joins me in sending her best to the both of you.

Your
Claude Monet

LW 2678

Letter from Clemenceau to Monet

Saint-Vincent, October 8, 24

My Old Heart,

Your letter pained me very much. Not because I believe all the things you say against yourself, for if you have created your masterpieces it is only because you were able to say the worst things about them. What pains me today is that there is so little reason in your reasoning. For children and for old men, we make excuses as long as we can. But there is a limit which should not be overstepped.

First you wanted to finish up some unfinished parts. It was not very necessary, but it was understandable. And then you got the absurd idea of improving the others. Who knows better than

you that a painter's impressions change all the time? If you went back to the cathedral of Rouen with your canvases, what would you not find to change? You created some new canvases, most of which were and still are masterpieces if you have not spoiled them. Then you wanted to make some *super-masterpieces,* and this with an instrument of sight that was imperfect because you yourself wanted it so.

And then you get angry at the idea that you will never be able to satisfy yourself. It is pure aberration. A true artist is never satisfied—you known that anyway. You have almost reached the end of the great journey. Whatever you do, you will leave behind the name of a painter who saw and felt the intimacy of things otherwise and better than anyone else had done before. You have the justifiable ambition of surpassing yourself, as much in your expression as in your sensations, and *you have done so.*

We have *seen* it, we *know* it, and at your request a contract was passed between you and *France,* in which the State has met all of its obligations. You have asked for the *postponement* of yours, and with my intervention, *it was granted to you.* Me, I have been of good faith, and I would not like to be taken, because of you, for someone who has done a disservice to art and to France in order to satisfy the whim of his friend. On your account the State is obliged to go to great expense, because of what you requested and even approved *in person.* You must therefore make an end of it, artistically and honorably, for there are no *ifs* in the commitments which you have made.

Only a true friend can spell things out so clearly. I am telling them to you, therefore, out of duty to you and to myself. That having been done, I ask you to let yourself be guided for once in your life by the advice of a friend who admires you as much and more than anyone else in the world, and who loves you dearly besides. Do you think that your honor as a painter is less dear to me than to yourself? Do you believe me capable of diminishing you in any way whatsoever? No, but you tell yourself that we are inferior judges, I and all the others who make the same speech. Well, I would reply that you are a bad judge of your judgment. I would reply that the judgment which you oppose to ours is undermined by the crazy venture of wanting to start a finished work all over again.

This, great friend of my heart, is what I had to tell you, because I love you enough to put you in front of the truth, at the risk of provoking those fits of irritation in which you indulge too readily, like a spoiled child.

If you will forgive my having done so, I will remain at your side. If not, you will never be able to keep me from loving you.

On Sunday, October 19, I will come to invite you for lunch. I arrive in Paris on the 16th in the evening.

Yours always.

G. Clemenceau

Corr. Clem., p.158

Letter from Clemenceau to Monet

Paris, January 7, 1925

My Unfortunate Friend,

However old, time-worn, he may be, artist or not, no man has the right to forego his word of honor—especially when it was to France that he gave his word.

I was going to write you to ask to have lunch with you on Sunday. But I give up absolutely, and if you keep to your mad decision, then I will have to take one of my own which may be more painful for me than for you.

By writing to Léon, without even letting me know, you have tried, like all weak men, to burn your bridges behind you. It was an offense which my friendship did not deserve. I knew that you were capable of doing crazy things. But I had not foreseen this. You speak of damages to the State! How wretched. It is to yourself that, by a crazy whim, you are doing the greatest harm!

You are old and your sight is failing. But you still have your genius. You want to make a misfortune out of this for yourself. This cruel caprice will have to do without my consent.

If your sight is failing, it is because *you wanted it so,* by letting the condition of your operated eye worsen and by refusing, like a mischievous child, to have the other one operated. And yet a veritable miracle took place. You were able to paint, and you did paint, more superbly and beautifully than ever before. As for the rest, there is no need for me to remind you. Your conscience, a victim of your own doing, will not let you forget until your dying breath. I am telling you the bare truth, for I have no more scruples with you.

And now the delirium of a spoiled child has taken hold of you. You have decided that your painting was worthless, even though all who have seen the panels declare them to be incomparable masterpieces, *even though you were pleased with them at our last meeting,* you cynically take back your word, declaring that even confirmed by your signature, it is worth zero. I would be dishonoring myself in turn if I were to argue with you the question which this raises. You wrote to me in Vendée: *"Come what may, my word will be kept."* That's the point at which I was regarding your promises; and I will not let myself be budged from it. If I had love for you, it was because I had given myself to the *you* that I saw you to be. If you are no longer this *you,* then I will remain an admirer of your painting, but my friendship will have nothing to do with this new *you.* I, too, am old and I have received hard knocks, but they have not diminished me in my own eyes. My ambition for you was that you be able to say the same.

G. Clemenceau

Corr. Clem., p.162

Letter from Monet to Dr. Mawas

Giverny-par-Vernon, Eure
March 25, 25

Dear Doctor

I am quite late in giving you news and the results of my new glasses. But I received them at a very bad time—very discouraged and not believing in any better results—and so I did not persist in using these glasses, to which I might have become accustomed, but which troubled me completely—troubled vision, the slightest tones separated and exaggerated.

As soon as I am better disposed, I will try to get used to them, although I am certain more than ever that the sight of a painter can never be regained. When a singer has lost his voice, he withdraws; the painter who has been operated for a cataract must give up painting: and that is what I have been unable to do.

Please excuse my frankness and believe in my sincere gratitude.

Claude Monet

LW 2596

Letter from Monet to Marc Elder

Giverny-par-Vernon
May 22, 1925

Dear Friend,

I received your precious package and sampled it with due serenity just as soon after. Result: it is delicious and you may congratulate your father-in-law. And thank you for having sent it to me.

I give you my thanks and urge you to believe me when I say that we are very touched by the friendship that you have shown to me and to my stepdaughter during this trying time for us.

As for me, I am absolutely overwhelmed by the passing away of so many loved ones. It is really very hard.

Excuse me and believe in my sincere friendship and in our best wishes for an improvement in your dear wife's health.

Mme. J. Monet was so touched by the letter which she received from her, but I don't even know what I am writing. I am no longer good for anything.

Your Friend,
Claude Monet

LW 2681

Letter from Monet to Marc Elder

Giverny-par-Vernon, Eure
October 16, 1925

Dear Friend,

Do not worry about your book, I received it from Gaston. I thanked him for it. I hope he received the letter.

All my thanks to you even though you make me say too much nonsense, but that is my fault. Too often I let myself repeat a bunch of memories that are more or less exact (?).

You probably already know that I have recovered my true sight and that this is like a new lease on life for me, and that I have gone back to work out of doors with an unparalleled joy and I am finally giving the finishing touches to my decorations. If I were not so busy (?) I would tell you to come to see me right away, but I do not want to lose a minute as long as I have not delivered my painting.

With best wishes to the two of you and until soon anyway.

Yours

Claude Monet

LW 2683

Letter from Clemenceau to Monet

Paris, February 8, 1926

Dear Good Friend,

If our bookkeeping were in order, it would be up to me to thank you all day long for so many wonderful works, so magnificently crowned. And what could I say of your good friendship? I am better. I may be able to go and see you before the end of February. I was very glad to hear that the first shipment needed only *"for the paint to dry"*. And when you say that you are *very pleased,* that means something. I understand you better than you think, for I am very hard to satisfy myself. May Demosthenes not cause you to yawn too hard.

The old man and the angel in my arms.

G. Clemenceau

Corr. Clem., p.177

Letter from Monet to Clemenceau

September 18, 1926

Dear and Good Friend,

It is finally me writing to you, happy to be able to tell you that I am better (although I am in great pain at times), but I am reasonable, I am recovering my appetite, [sic] that I sleep fairly well thanks to the care of Ribière and of Doctor Florand so much so that I am thinking of preparing my brushes and palette to take up my work again unless a relapse or too much pain keep me from doing it. I do not lose courage for all that and am taking care of great changes in my studio and plans for improving the garden.

All of this to say that I am back on top of things with courage.

Can you read all this verbiage? I hope so and hope also that we will soon have your visit, which will help me get back on my feet completely. Finally, know that if I do not regain sufficient strength to do what I want to my panels, I have decided to give them as they are or at least in part.

And you, how are you doing. Better than me I hope. I embrace you with all my heart.

Blanche and Michel join themselves to me.

Yours more than ever.

Claude Monet

LW 2685

Claude Monet at Giverny,
in his parlor-studio

Official Documents

April 12, 1922
Donation by Claude Monet to the French State

(Décember 30, 1922
Waiver of the notification of acceptance of the donation)
Offices of Maître Baudrez, notary, in Vernon (Eure)

Before Maître Gaston Henri Baudrez, the undersigned notary in Vernon (Eure),
   In the presence of:
   Mr. Louis Alphonse Laniel, attorney, member of the County Council of l'Eure and Mayor of the Town of Vernon, residing at 1, rue d'Albufera.
   And Mr. Francois Burthe, attorney in Paris, residing at 43, avenue Kléber.
   Witnesses to the deed as required by law.

Appeared

Mr. Claude Oscar Monet, artist, residing in Giverny.

Having by this deed donated *inter vivos* and irrevocably to the French State, in full ownership, his personal works hereinafter described, which form a collection of nineteen decorative panels, known as the "The Nymphéas Series", listed below:
   For a first room.
1. The Clouds. Three (3) panels of four meters twenty-five centimeters (4.25 m.) each.
2. Morning. Three (3) panels of four meters twenty-five centimeters (4.25 m.) each.
3. Green Reflections. Two (2) panels of four meters twenty-five centimeters (4.25 m.) each.
4. Setting Sun. One (1) panel of six (6) meters.
Total: nine (9) panels.
   For a second room.
1. The Three Willows. Four (4) panels of four meters twenty-five centimeters (4.25 m.) each.
2. Morning. Four (4) panels (separate) of six (6) meters each.
3. Tree Reflections. Two (2) panels of twenty-four centimeters (4.25 m.) each.
Total: ten (10).
Complete total: nineteen (19) panels.
Thus ten (10) compositions.

   However, Mr. Claude Monet reserves the exclusive right to make any modifications or changes he deems necessary, up to the date at which the physical transfer of the donated panels will take place, as indicated hereinafter.

   The French State is the legal owner of the panels from this day on, except for the modifications that the donor reserves the right to make.

   If any modifications are made by the donor, they must be recorded in an official deed by a notary on the date of the physical transfer of the panels to the State.

Charges and conditions

The present donation is made under the following charges and conditions which are deemed essential and without which the donation would not occur. The French State is explicitly obligated to abide by and fulfill said charges and conditions, namely:

1° The French State will accept delivery of the donated panels in their actual condition whether good or bad, the donor furnishing no guarantee, on the date of taking possession as set forth hereinafter in paragraph three.

2° The donated works will be used for the sole purpose of creating a Claude Monet Museum in the building of the Orangerie in the Tuileries, two rooms to be assigned to the panels herein described, to the exclusion of any paintings or sculpture.

3° The donated works will be delivered to the State as soon as installations for their proper display have been completed at the Orangerie of the Tuileries.

   These installations must be built according to the plans established on January twenty, nineteen hundred and twenty-two by Mr. Lefèvre, architect, said plans will remain attached hereto.

The entire costs of these installations will be incurred by the State, which guarantees that the work will be completed at the very latest two years from the date of provisional acceptance.

4° Under no circumstance shall the arrangement of the donated panels be modified in any manner.

5° The canvases of the paintings in the present donation shall never be varnished.

Rescission and cancellation clause

In the absence of a definitive acceptance of the donated property by the French State within six months, the present donation will be rescinded *ipso jure*.

   In the event of non-compliance, duly established, to any or all of the clauses and conditions set forth herein, the present donation will be cancelled forthwith.

Declaration of civil status

Mr. Claude Monet states that he is a widower and that he is the father of one male child of legal age.

Provisional acceptance

Party joining in the present deed:
   Mr. Paul Léon, Director of the Beaux-Arts, Officer of the Legion of Honor, residing in Paris at 3, rue de Valois, acting in said capacity, after having read the preceding donation, declares that he accepts said donation on a provisional basis, subject to the charges and conditions contained herein, as required by article nine of the law of February four, nineteen hundred and one.

   This donation will become final only after acceptance by the official duly authorized by the decree of acceptance.

   Mr. Claude Monet states that he agrees to the provisional acceptance set forth herein and formally dispenses Mr. Paul Léon of his obligation to notify him of the final acceptance of the present donation.

Valuation

To fulfill the requirements of article nine hundred and forty-eight of the Civil Code, the set of donated panels listed herein is valued at the sum of one hundred thousand francs.

Costs

The costs of the present deed and of the subsequent legal instruments will be incurred by the French State.

Acknowledgement

Executed and signed in Vernon, in the offices of the undersigned notary at 75, rue d'Albufera.
   The year nineteen hundred and twenty-two. April twelve.
   After the reading of the deed, Mr. Claude Monet signed with Mr. Paul Léon, the witnesses and the notaries.

   The witnesses were physically present when the notary read the deed and the parties signed as required by law.

   Claude Monet, Paul Léon, L. Lamel, Burthe, Baudrez.

   Initialed in lieu of stamp. April fourteen, 1922.
   8312. Gratis.

Before Maître Gaston Henri Baudrez, the undersigned notary in Vernon (Eure).
   In the presence of:
   Mr. Jules Louis Fernand Maréchal, attorney practicing at the Civil Court of Saint-Quentin, residing in Vernon at 13, avenue Gambetta.
   And Mr. Alexandre Alfred Guillaume, violin-maker, residing in Vernon at 76, rue d'Albufera.
   Witnesses to the deed as required by law.

Appeared

Mr. Claude Oscar Monet, artist, residing in Giverny.

Having acknowledged after the reading by Maître Baudrez, the undersigned notary, the authentic copy attached herewith of a deed recorded by Maître Burthe and Amy notaries in Paris on December four, nineteen hundred and twenty-two, stipulating that Mr. Léon Bérard, Minister of Public Instruction and Fine Arts, residing in Paris in the Hôtel du Ministère, 110, rue de Grenelle, acting in the capacity of Minister of Public Instruction and Fine Arts and as a representative of the French State, and in view of the decree of authorization issued by the President of the French Republic on June four, nineteen hundred and twenty-two, has explicitly accepted the donation to the French State for the Musées Nationaux by the party appearing presently, of a collection of personal works in accordance with the deed signed in the presence of Maître Baudrez, the undersigned notary, on April twelve, nineteen hundred and twenty-two, a copy of which precedes.

Has hereby stated that he is in agreement with the form of acceptance employed herein and considers the donation to be duly notified and therefore waives the State's obligation to notify him by process server.

Mention of this document is authorized wherever necessary.

Acknowledgement: written on unstamped paper as prescribed by the laws of Frimaire twenty-two [Dec. 11, 1797] and Brumaire thirteen [Nov. 3, 1798] of the year seven.

Executed and signed in Vernon, 75, rue d'Albufera, in the offices of the undersigned notary.

The year nineteen hundred and twenty-two. December thirty.

After the reading of the deed, the appearing party signed with the witnesses and Maître Baudrez, notary (the witnesses being physically present when the notary read the document and the parties signed, as required by law).

Claude Monet, Maréchal, A. Guillaume, Baudrez.

Initialed in lieu of stamp. January four, 1923.
2814 Gratis.

Before Maître Francois Burthe and Maître Amy, the undersigned both being notaries in Paris.

Appeared
Mr. Léon Bérard, Minister of Public Instruction and Fine Arts, residing in Paris, in the Hôtel du Ministére, 110, rue de Grenelle.

Acting in the capacity of Minister of Public Instruction and Fine Arts, and specifically authorized to negotiate the present deed, by virtue of a decree issued by The President of the French Republic in Paris on June four, nineteen hundred and twenty-two, a copy of which is attached herewith.

Having in his capacity acquainted himself by his own reading and by that of Maître Burthe, one of the undersigned notaries, with a deed recorded by Maître Baudrez, notary in Vernon (Eure), on April twelve, nineteen twenty-two, in the physical presence of the witnesses, according to which Mr. Claude Cesar [sic] Monet, artist, residing in Giverny (Eure) has donated *inter vivos* and irrevocably to the French State, as set forth in the aforementioned deed, a collection of personal works consisting of ten compositions forming nineteen panels valued at the total sum of one hundred thousand francs.

Has declared having accepted the donation mentioned herein without reservations or restrictions and definitively. Further declaring that all the clauses and stipulations will be enforced, in accordance with the aforementioned decree attached hereto.

Costs
All costs for the present deed will be incurred by the French State as engaged by the authority of Mr. Léon Bérard.

Acknowledgement
Executed and signed in Paris, 110, rue de Grenelle in the office of the Minister of Public Instruction.

The year nineteen hundred and twenty-two. December four.

And after the reading, Mr. Léon Bérard signed with the notaries.

The reading of the present deed by Maître Burthe and the signing by Mr. Léon Bérard, took place in the physical presence of Maître Amy, second notary, as required by law.

The recording information and signatures follow below.

Recorded in Paris, 14ᵉ notaries-December nine, nineteen hundred and twenty-two.

Volume: 13 A; Folio: 8 5; division: 3.
Received: gratis
Signed: Richelet
Burthe
Paris, December 15, 1922
Jais

Decree

The President of the Republic of France
Based on the report of the Minister of Public Instruction and Fine Arts.

In view of the notarized deed date April 12,1922 according to which Mr. Monet, Claude Oscar, artist, residing in Giverny, has donated works of art to the State under certain conditions, in view of article 910 of the Civil Code and the law of February 4, 1901; after having heard the Interior, the Public Instruction and the Fine Arts sections of the *Conseil d'Etat;*

Decrees:

Article one
The Minister of Public Instruction and Fine Arts is authorized to accept, in the name of the State and with the clauses and conditions stated, the donation made to it by Claude Monet under the terms of the deed signed above and consisting of a collection of personal works of art comprising ten compositions forming nineteen panels valued at the total sum of one hundred thousand francs.

Article two
The Minister of Public Instruction and Fine Arts is responsible for the application of the present decree, which will be published in the *Journal Officiel* and in *the Bulletin des Lois*

Executed in Paris, June 14, 1922.
By the President of the Republic
signed: A. Millerand
The Minister of Public Instruction and Fine Arts:
signed: Léon Bérard.
(Translated by François Miller)

126

Micrographic analysis
of the pigments and support

Identification
of the principal pigments

Laboratory analyses have identified the following sequence of layers: on the plaster of the wall: a thin covering composed of a coat of zinc white in oil. After, there is the mounting layer itself, a homogeneous mixture of glue, white lead, and oil about 3/10 mm. thick.
Next, there is the canvas, then a preparation of white lead and oil, and then the paint film. The detail of the structure of the support is illustrated by the following section.

The pigments were analyzed by Microfluorescence-X and complemented by microchemical tests.

Golden yellow: Cadmium yellow + lead white.
Light green: chrome green + zinc white.
White: lead white.
Light pink: lead white + small quantities of organic red pigment well mixed with the white.
Dark blue: lead white + cobalt blue (aluminate).
Ultramarine: artificial ultramarine + some cobalt blue + some lead white and zinc white.
Violet: cobalt violet (arsenate).
Dark green: chrome green + zinc white.

All of the colors were made out of very finely-ground pigments mixed with the oil medium.

1 Plaster.
2 Plaster slightly impregnated with glue.
3 Thin white coat (approx. 60 Ĭm.). Zinc white mixed with pure oil.
4 Thick white coat for the mounting of the canvas (approx. 300 Ĭm.). Mixture of white lead, glue, and oil. Very homogeneous mixture containing more glue than oil.
5 Glued canvas. Thin surface coat of pure glue.
6 White ground (50 to 100 Ĭm thick). White lead and oil. Perhaps a small amount of glue.
7 Paint film of very irregular thickness, mixed with oil.

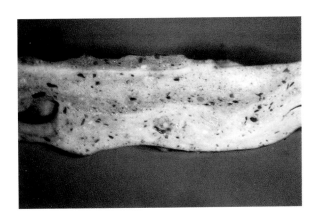

Stratigraphy sample of the pictorial layer. The superposition of many layers of pigment in this impasto shows Monet's progressive working up and retouching.

J.-P. Rioux and S. Delbourgo

Bibliography

Books on the *Nymphéas*

Aïtken, Geneviève et Delafond, Marianne
La collection d'estampes japonaises de Claude Monet à Giverny, préface de G. Van der Kemp, Paris, 1983.

Alphant, Marianne
Claude Monet: une vie dans le paysage. Paris, Hazan, 1993.

Claudel, Paul
Journal, T.I., p. 778 (July 1927), Paris, 1968.

Clemenceau, Georges
Claude Monet. Les Nymphéas. Paris, 1928.

Clemenceau, Georges
Georges Clemenceau à son ami Claude Monet: correspondance. Paris, 1993.

Degand, Léon and Rouart, Denis
Monet. Geneva, 1958.

Dufwa, Jacques
Winds from the East. Stockholm, 1982.

Elder, Marc
A Giverny chez Claude Monet. Paris, 1924.

Fels, Marthe de
La vie de Claude Monet. Paris, 1929.

Geelhaar, Christian (with contributions by G. Boehm, F. Meyer, A. Schmidt and R.T. Stool)
Claude Monet, Impression-Vision, Paris, Seghers, 1988 (French version of the catalogue from the exhibition at the Kunstmuseum of Basle, 1986).

Geffroy, Gustave
Claude Monet, sa vie, son temps, son œuvre. Paris, 1922, re-ed. 1924; *Claude Monet, sa vie, son œuvre;* re-ed. presented by C. Judrin. Paris, 1980.

Georgel, Pierre
Claude Monet: Nymphéas. Paris, 1999.

Georgel, Pierre
Monet: le Cycle des "Nymphéas". Paris, 1999.

Georgel, Pierre
Monet: les Nymphéas. Paris, 2006.

Gillet, Louis
Trois variations sur Claude Monet. Paris, 1927

(Selection of articles, the first appeared in *La Revue hebdomadaire* of Aug. 21, 1909).

Gimpel, René
Journal d'un collectionneur, marchand de tableaux. Paris, 1963.

Gordon, Robert and Forge, Andrew
Monet, New York, 1983.

Grappe, Georges
Monet. Paris, 1941.

Gwynn, Stephen
Claude Monet and His Garden. London, 1934.

Hoschedé, Jean-Pierre
Claude Monet, ce mal connu. 2 Vols. Geneva, 1960.

House, John
Monet, Nature into Art, New Haven and London, 1986.

Isaacson, Joël
Claude Monet, Observation et réflexion. Neuchâtel, 1978.

Joyes, Claire
Claude Monet et Giverny, preface by Gerald Van der Kemp, Paris, 1985.

Joyes, Claire; Gordon, Robert; Toulgouat, Jean-Marie; and Forge, Andrew
Monet at Giverny, London, 1975.

Keller, Horst
Ein Garten wird Malerei – Monets Jahre in Giverny. Cologne, 1922.

Levine, Steven Z.
Monet and His Critics. New York and London, 1976.

Levine, Steven Z.
Monet, Narcissus, and Self-Reflection: the Modernist Myth of the Self. Chicago, 1994.

Manet, Julie
Journal 1893-1899. Paris, 1979.

Martet, Jean
Monsieur Clemenceau peint par lui-même. Paris, 1929.

Masson, André
Le plaisir de peindre. Paris, 1950, pp. 61-62.

Mauclair, Camille
Claude Monet. Paris, 1924. London 1927.

Mount, Charles Merril
Monet, New York, 1966.

Murray, Elizabeth
Monet's Passion: ideas, inspiration and insights from the painter's gardens. San Francisco, 1989.

Patin, Sylvie
Monet: "un œil... mais, bon Dieu, quel œil!". Paris, 1991.

Patin, Sylvie
Regards sur les Nymphéas, Paris, 1996.

Rouart, Denis; Rey, Jean-Dominique; and Maillard, Robert
Monet, Nymphéas ou les miroirs du temps. Paris, 1972.

Sagner-Düchting, Karin
Claude Monet, "Nymphéas", eine Annäherung, Hildesheim, Georg Olms, 1985.

Sagner-Düchting, Karin
Claude Monet und die Moderne. Munich, 2001.

Schneider, Pierre
Petite Histoire de l'infini en peinture. Paris, 2001.

Seitz, W.C.
Claude Monet. New York, 1960, French ed. 1966.

Spate Virginia
Claude Monet. Life and Work. New York, 1992 (French translation: *Claude Monet: la Couleur du temps.* Paris, 1993).

Stuckey Charles F.
Claude Monet 1840-1926. Chicago - London, 1995.

Stuckey Charles F.
Monet: Waterlilies, New York, 1988 (French translation: *Claude Monet: Nymphéas,* Paris, 1995).

Suares, Georges
La vie orgueilleuse de Clemenceau. Paris, 1930, pp. 620 to 627.

Tucker, Paul Hayes
Claude Monet: Life and Art. New Haven - London, 1995.

Tucker, Paul Hayes *et al.*
Monet in the 20th Century. Boston - London, 1998.

Van der Kemp, Gérald
Une visite a Giverny. n.p., 1980.

Venturi, Lionello
Les archives de l'Impressionnisme. Paris - New York, 1939.

Walter, Rodolphe
Le Médecin de Claude Monet, Jean Rebière, Paris, 1986.

Wildenstein, Daniel
Claude Monet, Paris, 1971.

Wildenstein, Daniel
Monet ou le Triomphe de l'Impressionnisme, followed by *Monet: Catalogue raisonné,* 4 vol., Cologne, 1996 (new edition of Daniel Wildenstein, *Claude Monet: Biographie et Catalogue raisonné,* 5 vol., Lausanne, 974-1991).

Zambianchi, Claudio
La Fin de son art: Claude Monet e le Ninfee dell'Orangerie. Turin, 2000.

Articles

Adhémar, Hélène
"Les Nymphéas" de Monet… and "Clemenceau", *Le Figaro littéraire,* No. 1099, 8 May 1967.

Alexandre, Arsène
"Le jardin de Monet", *Le Figaro* 9 August 1901.

Alexandre, Arsène
"Claude Monet", *Le Figaro,* 6 Nov. 1921.

Bachelard, Gaston
"Les Nymphéas ou les surprises d'une aube d'été", *Verve* VII. no. 27-28 Dec. 1952, pp. 59-64.

Barotte, René
"Blanche Hoschedé nous parle de Claude Monet", *Le Figaro,* 24 Oct. 1942.

Blanche, Jacques-Emile "Claude Monet", *Les Nouvelles littéraires,* 18 Apr. 1931.

Blume, Mary
"The gardener of Giverny" *Art News,* Apr. 1978.

Breuil, Félix
"Les iris aux bords des eaux" *Jardinage,* 21 Oct. 1913.

Butor, Michel
"Claude Monet ou le monde renversé". *Art de France,* III, 1963, pp. 277-300.

Charvet, Louis
"Oraison funèbre pour Claude Monet", *La Revue des Jeunes,* 1927, pp. 85-93.

Connaissance des Arts, special issue, n° 137, 1999, "Monet, les Nymphéas"

Dittière, Monique
"Comment Monet recouvra la vue après l'opération de la cataracte", *Sandorama* n° 32, 1973, pp. 26-32.

Dossiers de l'art, no. 5, June 1999: "Le Cycle des Nymphéas".

Durand-Ruel, Charles
"Le destin des Nymphéas", *Connaissance des Arts* no. 366, 1980.

Escholier, Raymond
"Les Nymphéas de Claude Monet", *Le Figaro,* 19 Nov. 1922.

Faure, Jean-Louis
"Les sources impressionnistes de l'abstraction moderne", *Bulletin* de la Faculté des lettres de Strasbourg, May-June 1968, pp. 741-746.

Francis, H. Sam
"Claude Monet, water lilies", *Cleveland Museum Bulletin 4/,* Oct. 1960.

Gassier, Pierre
"Monet et Rodin photographiés chez eux en couleur", *Connaissance des Arts* no. 278, 1975, pp. 92-97.

Geffroy, Gustave
"Claude Monet", *Le Journal,* 7 June 1898 and *Le Gaulois,* 16 May 1898 (supplement).

George, Waldemar
"Les Nymphéas", *La Revue mondiale,* 15 June 1927.

Ghéon, Henri
"Les paysages d'eau de Claude Monet", *NRF VI,* 1909.

Gimpel, René
"At Giverny with Claude Monet", *Art in America,* no. 15, 1926-1927, pp. 168-174.

Giolkowska, Muriel
"Monet, his garden, his world", *International Studio,* no. 76, Feb. 1923, pp. 371-378.

Goldberg, Vicki
"Paintings from a garden", *Horizon,* Apr. 1978.

Gordon, Robert
"The lily pond at Giverny: the changing inspiration of Monet". *The Connoisseur,* Nov. 1973, pp. 153-165.

Gordon, Robert & Stuckey, Charles F.
"Blossoms and Blunders. Monet and the State"-I, *Art in America,* Jan.-Feb. 1979, no. 1, pp. 102-117.

Greenberg, Clement
"The latest Monet", *Art News Annual,* 1957 XXVI, pp. 132-148.

Guillemot, Maurice
"Claude Monet", *La Revue illustrée,* no. 13, 15 March 1898, n.p.

Hoelterhoff, Manuela
"Monet at Giverny: remarkable daring colour". *Wall Street Journal,* April 28, 1978.

Hoog, Michel
"La Cathédrale de Reims de Claude Monet ou le tableau impossible". *La Revue du Louvre,* Feb. 1981, no. 1, pp. 22-24.

Howard-Johnston, Paulette
"Une visite à Giverny en 1924", *L'ŒIL,* no. 171. March 1969, pp. 28, 33, 76.

Hughes, Robert
"The old man and the pond", *Time,* May 1978, pp. 79-71.

Johnston. J. Theodore (Jr.)
"Proust's "impressionism" Reconsidered in the

Light of the Visual Arts of the Twentieth Century",
*Twentieth Century French Fiction: Essays for
Germaine Brée*, New Brunswick. New Jersey,
Rutgers University Press, 1975, pp. 27-56.

Kahn, Maurice
"Le jardin de Claude Monet", *Le Temps*, 7 June 1904.

Levine, Steven Z. "Monet, lumière and cinematic
time", *The Journal of aesthetics and art criticism*
XXXVI/4, Summer 1978, pp. 441-447.

Marx, Roger
"Les Nymphéas de Monsieur Claude Monet",
GBA 1909, I, pp. 523-531.

Masson, André
"Monet le fondateur". *Verve* vol VII, no. 27 and 28,
1952, p. 68.

Mirbeau, Octave
"Claude Monet", *L'Art dans les deux mondes*,
7 March 1891.

Mirbeau, Octave
"Lettres à Claude Monet", *Les Cahiers d'aujourd'hui*,
no. 7, 29 Nov. 1922, pp. 161-176.

Nakayama K. and Kuroe M.
"Claude Monet dans les collections japonaises",
Bulletin annuel du Musée national d'art occidental,
no. 2, Tokyo, 1968.

Pays, Marcel
"Un don précieux", *L'Excelsior*, 16 May 1921.

Péguy, Charles
Clio, text of 1912, first published in *La Grande
Revue*. Oct. 1917. Pub. in book from Paris, n.d.
pp. 42-45 and 54-55.

Perry, Lilla Cabot
"Reminiscences of Claude Monet from 1889
to 1909", *The American Magazine of Art* XVIII, 3.
March 1927.

Pleynet, Marcellin
"Monet et les nouveaux héritiers", *Connaissance
des Arts*, no. 336, Feb. 1980, p. 3 and pp. 54-61.

René-Jean
"L'Impressionisme et Monsieur Claude Monet",
Comoedia, 11 Nov. 1922.

René-Jean
"Claude Monet est mort", *Comoedia*, 6 Dec. 1926.

Rey, Jean-Dominique
"Claude Monet, précurseur de l'abstraction
lyrique", *Plaisir de France*, Sept. 1971.

Rey, Jean-Dominique
"La dernière révolution: le spectateur, partie
intégrante de l'œuvre", *Galerie-Jardin des Arts*,
July-Aug. 1974.

Salomon, Jacques
"Chez Monet avec Vuillard et Roussel", *L'Œil*,
no. 197, May 1971, pp. 20-25.

Seitz, William C.
"Monet and abstract painting", *College Art Journal*
L. XVI, 1956, pp. 34-36.

Stuckey, Charles F.
"Blossoms and blunders: Monet and the State"-II.
Arts in America, no. 5, Sept. 1979. *Télérama*, special
issue, Summer 1999, p. 83.

Thiébault-Sisson
"Claude Monet, un entretien", *Le Temps*, 27 Nov.
1900.

Thiébault-Sisson
"Claude Monet", *Le Temps*, 6 Apr. 1920.

Thiébault-Sisson
"Un don de Monsieur Claude Monet à l'Etat",
Le Temps, 14 Oct. 1920.

Thiébault-Sisson
"Un nouveau musée parisien. Les Nymphéas
de Claude Monet à l'Orangerie des Tuileries",
La Revue de l'art ancien et moderne LII, June 1927,
pp. 41 - 52.

Toulgouat, P.
"Peintres américains à Giverny", *Rapports France-
États-Unis*, n° 62, May 1952.

Trévise, duc de
"Les quatre-vingts ans du peintre Claude Monet",
La vie aux champs, 15 Jan. 1921.

Trévise, duc de
"Le pèlerinage de Giverny", *La Revue de l'art ancien
et moderne*, special ed. 51), Jan.-Feb. 1927, pp. 42-50
and 121-134.

Truffaut, Georges
"Le jardin de Claude Monet", *Jardinage*, no. 87,
Nov. 1924.

Valbelle, Roger
"Ce qui se prépare au Musée Monet et au Musée
Rodin", *L'Excelsior*, 25 Dec. 1923 (?)

Vauxcelles, Louis
"Un après-midi chez Claude Monet", *L'art et les
artistes*, Dec. 1905.

Verne, Henri
"Le temple des Nymphéas", *Le Monde illustré*,
23 Oct. 1920.

Villemer, Jean
"Les Nymphéas de M. Claude Monet", *Le Gaulois*,
16 Oct. 1920 (?)

Wormser, André
"Claude Monet et Clemenceau: une singulière
amitié", in John Rewald and Frances Weitzenhoffer,
*Aspects of Monet: a symposium on the artist's life
and times*, New York, 1984.

Zürcher, Bernard
"L'effet Nymphéas", *L'art vivant* no. 2, May 1984,
pp. 14-15.

R. Gordon's book *Monet* came to our attention
only after the present work was finished and
at press.

Exhibitions

This is not an exhaustive list of the exhibitions of the works of Claude Monet. Of the older exhibitions, we have retained only those in which at least one Water Lilies subject was presented, and for the more recent exhibitions, only the most important or those whose catalogue (mentioned in the body of the text by the date and city) featured new source material. Although the first Water Lilies were unveiled at Durand-Ruel's gallery as early as 1900, it was a few years before they appeared in collective exhibitions. Thus, at the annual exhibition in Pittsbugh, in which Monet was regularly represented, the first Water Lilies were not shown before 1909. The same goes for the many Impressionist exhibitions held in Germany before 1914.

1900
Paris, Durand-Ruel, *Claude Monet*.
1901
New York, Durant-Ruel, *The Nymphéas*.
1904
Brussels, La libre esthétique, *Peintures impressionnistes*.
1905
Boston, Copley Society, *Monet-Rodin*.
1909
– Paris, Durand-Ruel, les *Nymphéas, Séries de paysages d'eau par Claude Monet*.
– Pittsburgh, Carnegie Institute, 13th Annual Exhibition.
1910
– Berlin, Secession.
– Leipzig, Kunstverein.
1912
Paris, Bernheim-Jeune, Preface by Octave Mirbeau, reprinted in des Artistes, 2e série, 1924, pp. 234-240.
1913
Munich, Glas Palast, Kunstaustellung.
1913
– New York, Armory Show.
– Rome, First International Secession.
1914
Pittsburgh, Carnegie Institute, 18th Annual Exhibition.
1915
San Francisco, International Exposition.
1918
Paris, Galerie Petit, 2nd Benefit Exhibition for the "Fraternité des artistes".
1921
Paris, Galerie Bernheim-Jeune, *Claude Monet*. Preface by A. Alexandre.
1924
– Paris, Galerie Georges Petit, *Hommage à Claude Monet*.

– New York, Durand-Ruel Gallery, *Water lilies by Claude Monet*.
1928
– Paris, Galerie Durand-Ruel, *Claude Monet*.
– Berlin, Tannhauser Galerie, *Claude Monet*.
1931
Paris, Orangerie, *Claude Monet*.
1936
– Paris, Galerie Durand-Ruel, *Claude Monet*.
– London, *Claude Monet*.
– Paris, Galerie P. Rosenberg, *Claude Monet*.
1939
London, *Claude Monet*.
1940
Paris, Orangerie, *Monet-Rodin*.
1942
Baltimore, Museum of Art, *Contrast in Impressionism*.
1945
New York, Wildenstein Gallery, *Monet*.
1952
Zurich, Kunsthaus, *Monet*.
1956
Paris, Galerie Katia Granoff, *Nymphéas de Claude Monet*.
1957
– Paris, Galerie Katia Granoff, *L'Etang enchanté de Claude Monet*.
– Edinburgh-London, *Claude Monet*.
1959
Paris, Galerie Art vivant, *Claude Monet et le naturalisme abstrait*.
1960
New York, Museum of Modern Art – Los Angeles County Museum, *Claude Monet, Seasons and Moments*.
1962
Basel, Beyeler Galerie, *Claude Monet, letzte Werke*.
1970
Paris, Galerie Durand-Ruel, *Claude Monet*.
1971
Paris, Musée Marmottan, *Monet et ses amis*, cat. by F. Daulte and Claude Richeblié.
1973
Tokyo, Kyoto, Fukuoka, *Claude Monet*.
1975
– Albi, Musée Toulouse-Lautrec, *Monet*.
– Chicago, Art Institute, *Painting by Monet*, text by André Masson "A propos de Claude Monet", from an interview by Alice Rewald.
1977-1978
Boston, Museum of Fine Arts, *Monet Unveiled*.
1978
New York, Metropolitan Museum, *Monet's Years*

at Giverny, texts by P. de Montebello, C. Moffet, J. Wood, D. Wildenstein.
1979
Ordrupgaard (Denmark) *Monet i. Giverny*, text by Hanne Finsen.
1980
Paris, Grand Palais, *Hommage à Claude Monet*, texts by A. Adhemar, A. Distel, S. Gache, M. Hoog.
1983
Paris, Centre culturel du Marais, *Claude Monet au temps de Giverny*, texts by M. Guillaud, J.-M. Toulgouat, C. Joyes, J. House, A. Baxter, P. Piguet.
1988
Ibaraki (Japan), Museum of Modern Art, *Monet and his Friends*.
1989-1990
Basle, Galerie Beyeler, *Claude Monet: Nymphéas*.
1992-1993
Paris, Musée de l'Orangerie, *Les Nymphéas avant et après*.
1994
Paris, Musée de l'Orangerie, *Les Nymphéas et Louis Cane*.
1995
– Chicago, The Art Institute of Chicago, *Claude Monet 1840-1926*.
– New Orleans, Museum of Art and San Francisco, The Fine Arts Museums, *Monet: Late paintings of Giverny from the Musée Marmottan*.
1998-1999
Boston, Museum of Fine Arts and London, Royal Academy of Arts, *Monet: in the 20th century*.
1999
Paris, Musée de l'Orangerie, *Monet: le cycle des Nymphéas*.
1999- 2000
Montréal, Musée des Beaux-Arts, Buffalo, Albright-Knox Art Gallery - Phoenix, Phoenix Art Museum, *Monet: peintures tardives de Giverny en provenance du musée Marmottan*.
2001
Munich, Kunsthalle der Hypo-Kulturstiftung, *Claude Monet und die Moderne*.
2001- 2002
Trevise, Casa dei Carraresi, *Monet: I luoghi della pittura*.
2002
Morioka (Japon), Iwate Museum of Art, Japan, *Monet Later Works: Homage to Katia Granoff*.
2004-2005
Brescia, Museo di Santa Giulia, *Monet, la Senna, le Ninfee: il grande fiume e il nuovo secolo*.

Index of names

The names of Monet and Clemenceau have been omitted.

Aïtken, Genevieve, p. 74
Ajalbert, Jean, pp. 15, 18
Alberti, Leon Battista, pp. 56, 69, 74
Alexandre, Arsène, pp. 18, 21, 22, 35, 38
Anquetin, Louis, p. 17
Aragon, Louis, p. 107

Bachelard, Gaston, pp. 7, 107
Barbier, André, pp. 15, 18
Bazaine, Jean, p. 96
Beckwith, Henry, p. 14
Benois, Alexandre, p. 39, 97
Bergson, Henri, p. 103
Bernheim-Jeune, Gaston and Josse, pp. 15, 16, 17, 121
Berthelot, Marcelin, p. 102
Bizet, Georges, 21
Blanche, Jacques-Emile, pp. 15, 17, 97
Blum Léon, p. 102
Bonnard, Pierre, pp. 18, 69, 96
Bonnier, Louis, pp. 24, 41, 43, 120
Borchardt, Félix, p. 18
Burty, Philippe, p. 11
Butler, Théodore, p. 14
Butor, Michel, p. 67, 91, 105

Caillebotte, Gustave, pp. 12, 13, 17
Camondo, Isaac de, p. 18
Carrière, Eugène, pp. 15, 18
Cathelineau, Mme, p. 18
Cézanne, Paul, pp. 11, 13, 14, 15, 17, 19, 69, 74, 100
Chagall, Marc, p. 6
Chaliapin, Feodor, p. 14
Chateaubriand, François-René de, p. 99
Chevreul, Michel, p. 102
Claudel, Paul, pp. 7, 32, 78, 96, 100, 101, 104, 107
Clemenceau, Paul, p. 15
Clémentel, Étienne, p. 16, 18, 50
Corot, Camille, p. 99, 102
Courbet, Gustave, pp. 74, 102
Coutela, Dr., pp. 50, 121
Crès, Georges, pp. 15, 18
Cross, Henri-Edmond, p. 99

Dante, pp. 26, 105
Degand, Léon, p. 96
Degas, p. 74
Delacroix, Eugène, pp. 17, 69, 76
Delafond, M., p. 74
Delaunay, Robert, pp. 17, 55, 76, 97, 99
Derain, André, p. 100
Descaves, Lucien, pp. 15, 18, 24
Deschanel, Paul, p. 24

Devéria, Eugène, p. 74
Diaghilev, Sergey, pp. 16
Durand-Ruel, Mme, p. 119
Durand-Ruel, Georges, pp. 17, 42, 119
Durand-Ruel, Joseph, p. 43
Durand-Ruel, Paul, pp. 6, 11, 17, 21, 42
Duret, Théodore, pp. 11, 17

Elder, Mme, p. 120, 121
Elder, Marc, pp. 50, 52, 121
Escholier, Raymond, pp. 76

Fantin-Latour, Henri, p. 11
Fels, Marthe de, p. 17
Flaubert, Gustave, p. 17
Florand, Dr., p. 124
Focillon, Henri, p. 15
Focillon, Victor, pp. 15, 18
France, Anatole, p. 18
Francis, Sam, p. 96
Fuller, Loïe, p. 14

Gache, Sylvie, p. 20
Gance, Abel, p. 56
Gallimard, Paul, p. 15
Gauguin, Paul, pp. 69, 99, 100
Gauthier, Théophile, p. 104
Geffroy, Gustave, pp. 12, 14, 15, 16, 17, 19, 42, 52, 76, 93, 101, 102
Georges-Michel, Michel, p. 18
Gervex, Henri, p. 42
Giacometti, Augusto, p. 100
Gillet, Louis, pp. 10, 13, 16, 17, 18, 21, 83, 94, 95, 104
Gimpel, René, pp. 18, 22
Gleizes, Albert, p. 97
Gleyre, Charles, pp. 19, 33
Goncourt, Edmond and Jules, p. 17
Gordon, Robert, p. 24, 41
Grappe, Georges, pp. 14, 16, 76
Guillaud, Maurice, p. 14, 15
Guillaume, Paul, p. 54
Guillemot, Maurice, pp. 18, 19, 20, 22
Guitry, Lucien, p. 18
Guitry, Sacha, pp. 16, 18
Guston, Philip, p. 96

Hamel, Maurice, pp. 15, 18
Helleu, Paul, p. 18
Helmholtz, Hermann von, p. 102
Hennique, Léon, pp. 15, 18
Hoschedé, Alice, pp. 17
Hoschedé, Blanche, pp. 53, 124
Hoschedé, Jean-Pierre, pp. 14, 17, 53
Hugo, Victor, pp. 19, 104
Huyghe, René, pp. 46, 48, 102, 103

Kahn, Gustave, p. 97
Kahn, Maurice, pp. 17, 18
Kandinsky, Wassily, pp. 56, 75, 76, 95, 102
Klimt, Gustav, p. 100
Kupka, Franti? ek, pp. 17, 76
Kuroki, Sadao, p. 18

Larionov, Michel, p. 76
Laurent-Fournier, *establishment* p. 53
Lefèvre, Camille, pp. 43, 45, 48
Léger, Fernand, p. 18, 100
Léon, Paul, pp. 41, 44, 120, 122
Levine, Steven Z., p. 56
Lhote, André, pp. 56, 97
Lissitky, Eliezer, p. 55
Loti, Pierre, p. 99
Louis, Morris, p. 96
Luce, Maximilien, p. 18

Maeterlinck, Maurice, p. 104
Malevitch, Casimir, pp. 75, 76
Mallarmé, Stéphane, p. 17
Manet, Edouard, pp. 11, 100
Marchiori, Giuseppe, p. 98
Margueritte, Paul, pp. 15, 18
Marquet, Albert, p. 99, 100
Marx, Roger, pp. 21, 107
Masson, André, pp. 7, 61, 94, 96
Mathieu, Georges, p. 96
Matisse, Henri, pp. 17, 107
Matsukata, Kójiró, p. 18
Mawas, Dr Lucien, pp. 52, 123
Metcalf, Willard Leroy, p. 17
Meyer-Schapiro, Ernest, p. 96
Michelangelo, pp. 61
Millais, Sir John Everett, p. 76
Millet, Jean-François, p. 99
Mirbeau, Octave, pp. 12, 15, 17, 94, 95, 97, 103, 104
Moffett, C., p. 55
Monet, Michel, pp. 120, 124
Mondrian, Piet, pp. 95
Monod, François, p. 54
Moore, George, p. 18
Moreau, Gustave, p. 105
Moreau-Nélaton, Etienne, p. 18, 23
Morisot, Berthe, pp. 15, 17

Natanson, Thadée, p. 17
Newmann, Barnett, p. 96
Noailles, Anna, comtesse de, p. 105

Ors, Eugenio d', pp. 56, 98
Ozenfant, Amédée, pp. 7, 107

Pavlova, p. 14
Pays, Marcel, pp. 14, 18, 42
Péguy, Charles, pp. 7, 21, 34, 104, 105, 107, 117
Perry, Lilla Cabot, pp. 14, 17
Picabia, Francis, p. 17
Picasso, Pablo, p. 17, 100
Pissarro, Camille, p. 18
Pissarro, Lucien, p. 18
Pollock, Jackson, p. 94, 96
Poussin, Nicolas, p. 105
Proust, Antonin, p. 11
Proust, Marcel, pp. 7, 31, 41, 102, 105, 106, 107
Puvis de Chavannes, Pierre, p. 15

Redon, Odilon, pp. 69, 100
Redouté, Pierre-Joseph, p. 104
Régamey, Raymond, pp. 96, 102
Régnier, Henri de, p. 106
Reinhardt, Ad., p. 96
Renard, Jules, p. 17
Renoir, Auguste, pp. 11, 13, 15, 17, 96
Restany, Pierre, p. 96
Rey Jean-Dominique, p. 96
Ribière, p. 124
Rimbaud, Arthur, p. 76
Riopelle, Jean-Paul, p. 62
Rivière, Georges, p. 96
Robinson, Théodore, pp. 14, 70
Rodin, Auguste, pp. 7, 11, 15, 16, 17, 20,
Rood, Ogden, p. 102
Rosny, J.H. senior, p. 15
Rousseau, Henri (Le Douanier), p. 100
Rousseau, Jean-Jacques, p. 99
Roussel, Ker-Xavier, p. 18
Ruskin, John, p. 105
Ryerson, Martin A., p. 18

Saleron, Germaine, p. 17
Sargent, John, pp. 15, 17
Seurat, Georges, pp. 99, 100, 102

Shakespeare, William, p. 76
Signac, Paul, pp. 17, 99, 102
Sisley, Alfred, pp. 11, 17
Stevens, Alfred, p. 11
Stevenson, Robert, p. 99
Still, Clifford, p. 96
Straus, Mme Emile, pp. 21, 105
Stuckey, Charles, pp. 41, 42
Sutton, J.F., pp. 21

Tarkhov, Nicolaï, p. 75
Teilhard de Chardin, Pierre, pp. 100, 101, 104
Thiebault-Sisson, François, pp. 7, 18, 22, 24
Tiepolo, Giovanni-Battista, p. 61
Tobey, Mark, p. 96
Toussaint, Abbot, p. 13
Trévise, Edouard, Mortier, duc de, pp. 18, 19
Turner, William, p. 98

Valéry, Paul, pp. 16, 18, 102
Van der Kemp, Mr. and Mrs., p. 7
Van Eyck, Jan, p. 56
Van Gogh, Théo, p. 17
Vaquez, Dr, pp. 15, 18
Vauxcelles, Louis, pp. 16, 17, 18
Venturi, Lionello, pp. 42, 43, 98
Vermeer, Johannes, p. 41
Verne, Henri, pp. 24, 53
Verne, Jules, p. 99
Veronese, Paul, p. 61
Villemer, Jean, p. 24
Vollard, Ambroise, pp. 100, 102
Vuillard, Edouard, p. 18

Wagner, Richard, p. 75
Walter, Mrs. Jean, p. 54
Whitman, Walt, p. 54
Wildenstein, Daniel, pp. 12

Zola Emile, pp. 11, 14, 17, 19, 102

Director of Publishing
Pierre Vallaud

Director of the Books Department
Catherine Marquet

Publication manager
Josette Grandazzi

Rereading
Isabel Ollivier

Production
Philippe Gournay

Graphic design and layout
Bruno Pfäffli

Photoengraving
Bussière, Paris

Printed and bound in Spain
by Ingoprint, Barcelona

Photographic Credits:

Grenoble, musée de Peinture et de Sculpture:
   p. 43
Le Havre, musées des beaux arts André-Malraux:
   p. 15
New York, The Museum of Modern Art © 2006 Digital Image,
The Museum of Modern Art/Scala:
   p. 101
Paris, Laboratoire de recherche des musées de France:
   p. 127
Paris, musée national d'Art moderne, centre Georges Pompidou
© CNAC/MNAM Dist. RMN:
   p. 94
Paris, musée Marmottan © The Bridgeman Art Library/Giraudon:
   p. 23, 53, 93
Paris, musée de l'Orangerie, documentation:
   p. 16 (left), 18, 46-47, 106
Paris, Réunion des musées nationaux
© All rights reserved:
   p. 8-9, 24 to 41, 56 to 59, 76 to 93
© Bulloz/RMN:
   p. 14
© H. Lewandowski:
   p. 53, 56
© D. Arnaudet:
   p. 21, 42, 48, 49, 97
Paris, Roger Viollet:
   p. 71, 72
Versailles, Art Lys/J. Girard:
   p. 16 (right)
Zurich, Kunsthaus:
   p. 103

1st Legal deposit November 1984
Legal deposit May 2006
ISBN 2-7118-5069-2
GA 20 5069